THE Cyclist's
BUCKET LIST

Also by Ian Dille:

The Price of Gold (With Marty Nothstein)

THE Cyclist's BUCKET LIST

A Celebration of **75** Quintessential
Cycling Experiences

IAN DILLE

RODALE.

Rodale books may be purchased for business or promotional use or for special sales. For information, please write to:
Special Markets Department, Rodale, Inc., 733 Third Avenue, New York, NY 10017

Printed in the United States of America

Rodale Inc. makes every effort to use acid-free ∞, recycled paper ♲.

Book design by Rae Ann Spitzenberger

Library of Congress Cataloging-in-Publication Data is on file with the publisher.

ISBN: 978–1–62336–446–5   hardcover

Distributed to the trade by Macmillan

2   4   6   8   10   9   7   5   3   1   hardcover

We inspire and enable people to improve their lives and the world around them.
rodalebooks.com

Contents

Europe

North America

UNITED STATES

Prologue

The bicycle, a human-powered machine of motion. Simple, really. Wheels. Pedals. Handlebars. Go. Through the city. To the park with your kids. Into the country-side, where cows stop chewing grass to look up (seemingly unimpressed), white-tailed deer scamper across the road, and hawks soar overhead, riding the very same wind gusts you do upon your bicycle. Up hills. Up mountains. And down, down, down, down.

Ridden to every end of the earth. Raced on dirt, and grass, and ice, and steeply sloped tracks, and around entire countries—even continents. Loved and fetishized. Broken up by style and discipline into clubs, and cliques, and cults. Put in museums, and hung from the ceilings of bars. Enshrined in churches. Prayed to.

All of this, not for the machine itself but for the experiences it engenders. Each experience unique to every ride and every rider. But inarguably, some experiences remain more memorable than others. The smell of lavender at a roadside picnic, waiting for the Tour de France to arrive. The vertigo-inducing view of the Pacific Ocean from the 10,000-foot summit of Hawaii's Haleakala volcanic crater (a 5-plus-hour climb). A crisp, pale lager hitting your lips after a ride along the canals of Amsterdam, one of the world's most bike-friendly cities. These are the sights, the smells, and the tastes that every cyclist should experience before they die.

These and a wide range of other must-do and -see rides, races, shops, and shrines, all rooted to a specific location or event, compose *The Cyclist's Bucket List*. This book is an entirely subjective attempt to catalog both the iconic and the little known—the accessible and aspirational—sensory and emotional experiences that instill in cyclists such passion for the sport. The siren song of roads that wind into the Alps, Dolomites, and Rockies and the death-defying descents deep in the Andes jungle. The unpredictable adventure of a multiday, or multimonth, bicycle tour across Vietnam, Patagonia, or Africa. Bike shops that serve as museums of the sport. Cities where bicycles overrule automobiles. Rides in traditionally uncelebrated places, like the cornfields of rural Iowa and the windswept Texas Panhandle, that draw thousands upon thousands of people. You'll read about these and many more in *The Cyclist's Bucket List*. And hopefully, you'll go experience them yourself before you die.

Ian Dille
October 2014
Austin, Texas

Africa

SUDAN

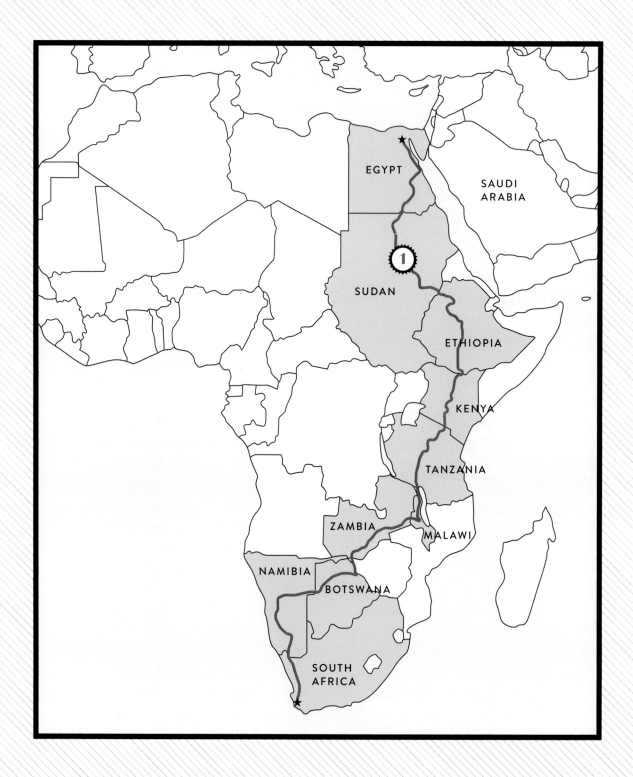

Tour d'Afrique

EGYPT TO SOUTH AFRICA

When Jenn Crake arrived in Egypt in January 2010, she felt prepared to ride her bike from Cairo to Cape Town, South Africa. She'd taken a 6-month leave of absence from her publishing career in Toronto to prepare for and complete the Tour d'Afrique and raised money for the entry fee ($14,500, plus another $20,000 for an African charity). She'd visited the head of the Tropical Disease Unit's clinic at the Toronto General Hospital to receive inoculations against various diseases—hepatitis A and B, typhoid, yellow fever, rabies, and half a dozen other potential maladies. She'd made a list, focusing on both comfort and economy.

Before she loaded her gear aboard the support truck that would follow her across the continent, it would be weighed. Her gear could not total more than 100 pounds. She spent extra money on nice cycling shorts and a comfortable seat ("saddle comfort is essential," she had written on her gear checklist), yet she brought only two pairs of pants ("which I would wear for a week at a time"). She bought a bike, a Kona Jake cyclocross bike, which she downgraded with low-end Shimano Alivio parts ("more likely to find replacement parts for in Africa") and equipped with Schwalbe Marathon Plus tires with super-duty flat protection to ward off knifelike thorns. (She got only five flats during her ride across Africa, but another rider on her trip patched a single inner tube 12 times.)

She trained diligently to prepare for the average 120 kilometers she would ride each day but concedes, "There is truly no way to prepare your body for 4 consecutive months of riding in Africa." Crake believed she had made every possible preparation, physically and logistically, but she failed to fully anticipate for the mental and emotional components of the trip. For the next 120 days she would be riding her bike more than at any other time in her life. She would sleep in a tent in the middle of some of the world's most uninhabited, and most inhabited, places. She would come to know complete strangers—the 50 other participants and half a dozen staff members who would also embark on this journey with her—better than people she had known her entire life.

> **As alone as a human can find himself or herself on this planet, Crake pedaled through a landscape inhabited by giraffes, gazelles, buffalos—and lions, jackals, and cheetahs.**

However, for Crake, the most disquieting, but also exhilarating, part of this ride across the world's largest continent was the realization that she would come to know *herself* better than ever before, too. She knew that at the completion of the Tour d'Afrique, she might no longer be the same person. Yet, she didn't know exactly who she would be. As she departed from Cairo, literally riding from the shadows of the pyramids out into a flat, brown landscape, the bright sun descending toward the vast Sahara Desert, a thought slowly dawned on her: *What the hell have I just done?*

The first Tour d'Afrique occurred in 2003, but the idea to ride across Africa from tip to tip had formed decades prior. Henry Gold, the man behind the seemingly mad event had traveled extensively in Africa as the executive director of Canadian Physicians for Aid and Relief. Based on his experiences there, Gold became convinced bicycles could prove transformative for the majority of people in Africa, but he struggled with how best to bring bikes and awareness to the continent.

During a trip to Ethiopia in the early '90s, he came across the Russian Olympic cycling team altitude-training in the mountains. A colleague, knowing Gold's inclination to tackle challenging projects, teased him that he should organize a bicycle race from the top of Africa to the bottom. Gold laughed, but days passed, and he couldn't get the idea out of his mind. So he went to a friend, Michael de Jong, an inventor and bike racer, and told him about the idea. De Jong became similarly fascinated with the Africa tour. De Jong planned a route and produced an informational brochure for potential participants.

They scheduled the first Tour d'Afrique for 1994, but a terrorist attack in Egypt forced them to cancel. The two men moved on, and the event went dormant for nearly 10 years. Then, on the eve of his 50th birthday, Gold found himself seeking a life-affirming challenge. He called de Jong, told him he wanted to do the Africa tour, and gave him 24 hours to decide. Eleven months later, the 2 men and 31 other participants, ranging from world-class adventurers to a 55-year-old mother of five who'd only begun riding that year, set off from Cairo and pedaled toward Cape Town.

Gold and de Jong had estimated the trip would take 120 days, with roughly 1 day of rest for every 5 days of riding. In order to garner additional press coverage and appease participants with competitive ambitions, the Tour d'Afrique was set up as (and officially remains) a race. Riders clock in individually at the start of each day and record their times at the finish. But racing is certainly not required. Packs of riders form pacelines and push for the finish each day while others dawdle, barely making it to camp before sunset. Many riders, including Crake, choose to race on certain days and ride more casually on others.

The first Tour d'Afrique participants, whom Gold believes were the first cyclists ever to ride across the continent consecutively, would serve as guinea pigs for the tours that followed. In Egypt, Sudan, Ethiopia, and Kenya, Gold had to depend on his previous good works in Africa and diplomatic connections to even gain access to the countries, which were in tense political conditions. Once south of Kenya, at the halfway point, they would rely solely on maps and local knowledge for guidance, as Gold had scouted the route only as far as Nairobi, the Kenyan capital.

Prior to his departure, Gold had listened to plenty of skepticism about the Tour d'Afrique: The ride was too long and logistically demanding for a large group; the continent was too poor and unstable; the roads were too rough, impassable by bike. But in May, the group—the world-class adventurers and the mother of five, who'd lost 30 pounds along the route—arrived in Cape Town an hour ahead of schedule. The accomplishment gained international coverage from such publications as the *New York Times*, *USA Today*, and Canada's national paper, the *Globe and Mail*.

Over time, Gold transformed the Tour d'Afrique into an international bike-touring company bearing the same name. The company offers ultra-distance tours around the globe. Though the Africa tour remains its most popular and best attended, the touring company offers supported trips across all seven continents—the Seven Epics, Gold calls them. Gold also figured out how to bring more bikes to the people of Africa. He formed the Tour d'Afrique Foundation, which donates a bicycle for every participant in the tour to communities along the route.

Crake hesitates to talk about her favorite moments, in a traditional sense, on the Tour d'Afrique. Sure, she experienced beauty and grandeur unlike anything she'd ever seen. But when she looks back on her ride across Africa, everything melds together, and it's her toughest days—the days that brought the deepest physical and emotional struggles—that remain the most poignant. Take, for example, Sudan, where the Tour d'Afrique crossed the 10,000-square-kilometer Dinder National Park for the first time at the invitation of the governor of the Sinnar province.

The deeper the riders went in the park, traversing rolling savannas and woodlands, the rougher the terrain became, until it proved almost impassable. Double-track dirt roads sank into deep sand, and gravel grew into boulders. The jaw-chattering washboard stretches spanned miles in front of the rider's wheels. Over half the group lost their EFI status (the acronym for Tour d'Afrique participants who cover "every f—ing inch" of the route without resorting to riding in the support truck). The day went down in Afrique history as the Dinder Disaster. Some riders, without hyperbole, referred to the Dinder ride as the worst day of their lives. Yet Crake, who also succumbed to the ignominious relief of completing the day in the support vehicle, recalls Dinder fondly, saying, "It was terrifying, but incredible." As alone as a human can find himself or herself on this planet, Crake pedaled through a landscape inhabited by giraffes, gazelles, buffalos—and lions, jackals, and cheetahs. Here, park residents forged an existence from the landscape and lived in thatch-roofed huts. "Remote Sudan felt like the place where time stood still," Crake says.

From Dinder, the Tour d'Afrique rises into the highlands of Ethiopia. Riders cross the Blue Nile Gorge, the headwaters of the mythic river that feeds all of northeast Africa, and partially circumnavigates Lake Tana, from which the Nile flows. During one 105-kilometer day, Crake tackled 2,250 meters of climbing, including a 20-kilometer switchback descent followed by a 20-kilometer climb.

By this point, Crake had also acquired gastrointestinal distress—an occurrence so common on the Tour d'Afrique that it is not a question of *when*, but rather, *how bad?* "Basically, at any one point during the Tour d'Afrique, to put it bluntly, one-third of the group is probably shitting themselves," says Crake. Still, diarrhea, dehydration, and mild flu rarely kept Crake off of her bike. When your stomach is in knots, she says, "Riding is often the preferred option to sitting in a truck over rough roads for 6 hours." In Ethiopia, a nation with a population of 91 million dispersed throughout the countryside, Crake struggled to find a moment of privacy. "It's so loud, there are people everywhere," she says. On her watch, she timed the longest stretch of quiet she encountered. It was 90 seconds.

Pedaling through Ethiopia, when Crake could no longer contain the gastrointestinal distress, she scanned the roadside for a discreet rest stop. "I would pull over and be like, 'There's no one here!' and pull my pants down, and suddenly there'd be 30 people standing around me. I was like, 'Where did you all come from? Seriously, where did you all just come from?'" Nevertheless, despite her stomach troubles, Crake in no way regrets gorging on the local foods of Sudan and Ethiopia—the injera flatbread, chickpea stew, and even *kitfo*, the spiced Ethiopian version of steak tartare. It was the best food she ate in all of Africa, she says.

The people of Ethiopia, whom Crake describes as some of the most beautiful people she saw on the entire trip, are unendingly fascinated with the Tour d'Afrique, a circus that rolls through their villages once a year. "Where are you go?" is the common refrain, shouted mostly by children. It's their way of asking where the riders are from, not necessarily where they are going.

Another, unfortunately common, interaction with children in Ethiopia involves rock-throwing. Crake says it's not entirely clear why the Ethiopian children throw rocks at Tour d'Afrique riders but that disparity in wealth and privilege certainly contribute. Crake calls these interactions, though negative, "a constant lesson" that forever expanded her capacity for patience and understanding. She could not apologize for her wealth, her education, her health care, her material possessions—all seemingly modest in her own country but lavish in comparison to many in Ethiopia, one of the world's most impoverished nations. Nor could she be disaffected by the reality of the situation. The experience, she says, made her a better human.

"These people have nothing. The poverty is very overwhelming," says Crake. She knew when heading to Africa that much of what she might see would make her sad, that it wasn't a tourist excursion, taking in only the noted sights and bypassing the bad. She would see all of eastern Africa, both the wonders and the horrors. "Fundraising for African charities was very important for me, because I knew that you can't, along the way, stop and give people anything," Crake says. "If you give one person something, you better give everyone something."

> **"Crake calls the Galgalu 'as remote as I'm probably going to be in my entire life. I'd go 4 hours before I'd see anyone else, before I'd run into another rider.'"**

At the camps in Ethiopia and Malawi, the Tour d'Afrique erects a perimeter, a simple rope around the outside that serves as an effective barrier, and hires local security. "Some people would come and just stand outside the perimeter, for like, 6 hours," Crake recalls. "You get used to that. Just being stared at all the time. You're sitting there, in your chair beside your tent, and there's 200 people standing around you. It's completely bizarre, like nothing I've experienced or will probably experience ever again." At one point, as she was eating, Crake broke down and turned her back on the people encircling the Tour d'Afrique camp. "It's so hard," she says. "If you don't eat, you don't ride. But these people are starving."

Ethiopia led to Kenya, bringing more surreal landscapes and inconceivably difficult terrain. The Tour d'Afrique is broken up into eight sections, and the company encourages riders to participate in this 1- to 2-week-long section if the entire trip is beyond their means or desire. They call the section across Kenya, with its 6 days of riding across the lava fields of the Dida Galgalu desert, Meltdown Madness. There are no turns, no detours, no bypasses in the desert. There's one road. In a video her friend made of the ride through the Galgalu, Crake—exhausted, delirious—stands on a road made of rocks the size of golf balls that extends into the foreseeable distance. "Here I am!" she exclaims. The next day, like in the movie *Groundhog Day*, Crake stands again on a road made of rocks the size of golf balls that extends into the foreseeable distance. "Here I am!" she says, again.

The Tour d'Afrique organizers state that the route is composed of roughly 20 percent dirt roads, with the rest paved (and increasingly so). Knowing this, Crake chose to ride a cyclocross bike, as many Tour d'Afrique participants do. The bike would be quicker and more comfortable than a mountain bike on the majority of paved roads but suitable enough for the dirt sections, she figured. Where the road got rough, she'd tough it out. However, 20 percent of a 12,000-kilometer trip is 2,400 kilometers of dirt roads in total. A day or so into the Galgalu, Crake was dreaming of full suspension.

"It's just blazing sun, there are no trees, just corrugation [washboard road] and sheer gravel. And the corrugation, it's just—you can't find a line in that, you can't get out of it. It's running against the grain. You're just constantly pounding away. Eight hours for 85 kilometers is probably the toughest riding that I can think of, and that

Get There

▸▸ The Tour d'Afrique entry fee covers 166 freshly prepared camp meals, 98 roadside lunches, and 1 meal in a restaurant. The accommodations include 2 nights in a hotel and 120 nights of camping. A medic, bike mechanic, and chef accompany the Tour d'Afrique for the duration of the journey, a tour leader provides details of each day's route, and a sweep rider makes sure no one gets left behind. Two support vehicles travel with the Tour d'Afrique, carrying riders' gear and food supplies and offering limited space for participants who're unable to ride. However, even with as much support as the Tour d'Afrique offers, a certain amount of self-reliance is critical. Riders set up and break down their own tents each day and take turns cleaning up after the dinner meal. Riders cover their own airfare to Africa and other amenities along the way, such as a safari tour on a rest day or a hotel or lodge stay when the Tour d'Afrique stops in a major city. The Tour d'Afrique provides riders with a basic equipment list, as well as information on the required vaccinations and visas. However, former participants are typically the best sources of information for what you'll need along the route, and many happily share their experiences via blogs or through personal contact. Visit tourdafrique.com for more information.

doesn't mean, *Oh, there were big hills*, it means, *Oh, I'm just trying to get over this rock*. The vehicles probably couldn't go as fast as the mountain bikes," Crake says. "Some people were taping their forearms."

Crake calls the Galgalu "as remote as I'm probably going to be in my entire life. I'd go 4 hours before I'd see anyone else, before I'd run into another rider."

From Nairobi, Kenya, Crake pedaled into Tanzania, riding beside the snow-capped volcanic peak of Africa's tallest mountain, the 5,895-meter Kilimanjaro. She rode through a landscape that seemed like a *National Geographic* stereotype of Africa, the land of big cats and wildebeest migrations, national parks and game reserves. In Arushu, considered east Africa's safari capital, the riders were given 3 days off. Crake took 2 days to go on safari and spent an evening in a hotel. A blessed hotel— after weeks of bathing with wet wipes or taking a sponge bath from a bucket and bedding down in her tent for the night.

On more dirt roads, over rolling terrain, she rode through the Maasai Steppe, past zebras and giraffes and red-cloaked Maasai tribesmen carrying spears and wearing plastic sunglasses. She rode through Malawi and Zambia, Botswana and Namibia, past banana plantations and beside farmers on heavy steel bicycles toting loads of grain and cages full of live chickens. She rode 6 centuries in 7 days on board-flat roads and saw elephants, hippos, and crocodiles. She descended into the Rift Valley, toward the turquoise water of Lake Malawi, and stood before Victoria Falls, the world's largest sheet of falling water. She took a break from her tent and spent a night at a lodge, eating her body weight in burgers and pancakes. On the eve of her 40th birthday, she leaned over the edge of the Fish River Canyon, 161 kilometers long and 550 meters deep, and recalls feeling "my entire body filled with pure joy."

Amid all the riding, the long, hot days and rough roads and sickness, Crake says the hardest part of the Tour d'Afrique for her was the people. The organizers of the Tour d'Afrique call it part expedition, part social experiment. "If you show up with any sort of mask, you'll quickly be revealed," Crake says. Pacelines became cliques. Friendships were formed and dissolved. Tents were apart one night, together the next. Love blossomed. Marriages followed. Relationships imploded (including Crake's own). Gossip was mongered. There was "business class," the group of driven middle-aged men who had their own locker stocked with red wine and fine cheeses and also donated more than 100 bikes to the Tour d'Afrique Foundation. (*How'd they*

get that locker? Crake and other tour riders wondered.) There was a woman who cried. Every. Single. Day. Some people gave up. Went home. Others, like a man with whom Crake became close friends, battled sickness for 3 of the tour's 4 months and still rode "every f—ing inch." The people were the hardest part for Crake, but she wouldn't have made it without them.

In May, she arrived in Cape Town, her bike barely functional. Many other riders were done with riding, at least for a while after the Tour d'Afrique. They donated their bikes to the Tour d'Afrique Foundation, sold them, or simply left them. Crake woke up the morning after riding across Africa and asked a staff member if she could borrow a bike. She rode up the coast, beside sandy beaches, and pedaled beneath Table Mountain, her mind wrestling with an entirely new and unexpected anxiety. How could she possibly return to a normal life?

For the past 4 months, Crake had done nothing but ride her bike and experience adventure. When she got back to Canada, she went straight to the bike shop and had her Kona overhauled. She had other bikes, sure, but she wanted to ride that one. Then, she rode to her cottage, 200 kilometers away. She kept thinking she should be in Africa. The gravitational force of the continent tugged at her.

Eventually, she reassimilated to her old life. She returned to work and didn't disappear on all-day bike rides quite as regularly. But she wasn't the same person. Her perspective on happiness had changed—and it didn't extend much beyond a functioning bicycle and a direction in which to pedal. Material possessions became less meaningful. Daily annoyances bothered her less. She admits that not everyone had her experience, cherishing the hard days the most—the sense of accomplishment they instilled, what they taught her about herself.

She warns anyone who's considering doing the Tour d'Afrique to be careful. Normal life may feel a little more boring. If you fall in love with this kind of adventure, you'll want to do more. Crake has since ridden in Mongolia and gone back to South Africa. She tries to take a major cycling trip every 2 years.

"The Tour d'Afrique may not change your life," says Crake. "But you better be prepared to deal with the consequences if it does."

Asia

LEH-MANALI HIGHWAY

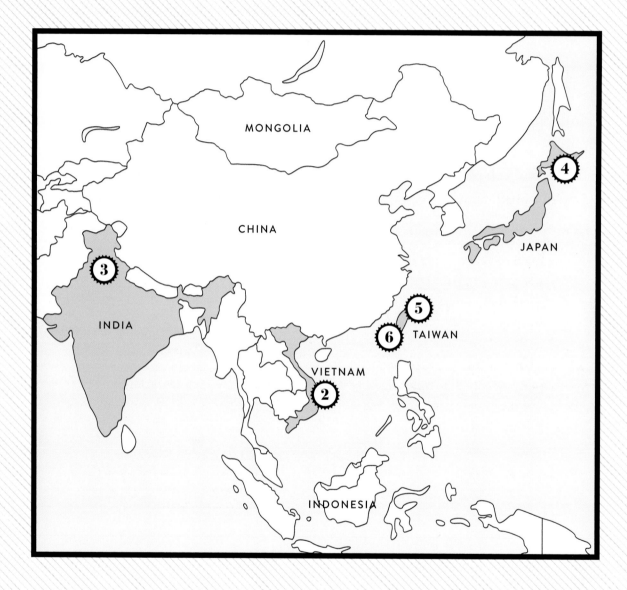

2

Highway 1

VIETNAM

From Hanoi to Ho Chi Minh City, Vietnam's Highway 1 spans more than 2,000 kilometers from north to south, unifying this once war-torn country. Long considered the lifeline of Vietnam and brutally bombed during the 1960s, the restored roadway borders vast stretches of pristine coastline, passes through both rural farmland and major cities, and intermittently ascends mountain passes overlooking the blue waters of the South China Sea. There's perhaps no better way to take in Vietnam's wide array of culture, food, and terrain than by traveling Highway 1. And there's no better way to travel Highway 1 than on a bike.

Get There

▸▸ A number of touring companies offer guided trips along Highway 1. One of the oldest and best regarded is Velo-Asia. For more than 20 years, VeloAsia has run a 12-day cycling tour along Highway 1 during Vietnam's Tet new year, when the roads are quietest. Velo-Asia's riding itinerary primarily focuses on the southern portion of Highway 1, between Hue and Ho Chi Minh City, but includes a diversion into the mountainous Central Highlands. Visit veloasia.com for more information.

③

Leh-Manali Highway

INDIA

Nothing really grows up here in the thin air near the top of the world. High in the Himalayas of northern India, in the Ladakh region, the town of Leh sits on the banks of the Indus River. The bare, windswept mountains rise from the earth in every direction, thrown into the air millions of years ago by the collision of the Indian and Eurasian tectonic plates. The shifting sun casts these rock-strewn peaks in shades of shining gold. The plates still shift, occasionally making these mountains shake. Thousands of people have forged a living in this remote landscape for thousands of years, despite constant conflict amongst various empires and the disparate interests of the nations we now know as Pakistan, China, and India. Today, the Indian Air Force maintains a military outpost in Leh and a firm grasp on the region.

Buddhism first came here in the 2nd century and found spiritual significance in the glacial waters of the Indus River winding through these Himalayan peaks, for where it flows, so does life. Juniper trees sprout from the river's banks, and fields of hearty produce, irrigated with the river's water, ripen during the few months without snow.

Get There

▸▸ A good resource for tackling the Leh–Manali highway is *Himalaya by Bike*, a guidebook with advice on pretrip planning, detailed route guides and maps, and accommodations along the road. Visit himalayabybike.com for more information. Additionally, a variety of outfitters offer supported tours of the Leh–Manali Highway, including luggage transportation, tent setup, and meals. Visit worldexpeditions.com for more information on its Himalayan cycling tours.

Upon the stone faces of the mountains surrounding Leh, the Buddhists built enthralling monasteries and temples.

If you come here to bicycle the highway connecting Leh in the barren northern Himalayas to Manali in the verdant south, one of the highest roads in the world, you will have plenty of time to explore these monasteries as you acclimate to the extreme altitude. Leh sits 3,000 meters above sea level, and the highway to Manali climbs farther, to 5,350 meters. The 12-story Thiksey Monastery, for example, with its ancient *thangkas* (intricate paintings on silk scrolls), is home to a 49-foot-tall statue of Maitreya (the future Buddha). You may need as much as a week in Leh to acclimate before partaking in this journey.

The 474-kilometer-long road to Manali follows the flow of the Indus River south, into the heart of the Himalayas. You'll ride past the Thiksey Monastery and toward the tiny village of Upshi, where the road forks right along a tributary of the Indus and begins a gradual 100-kilometer ascent toward the Taglang La pass. The elongated switchbacks of the Leh–Manali highway gently snake up the side of Taglang La, and the narrow road morphs from asphalt to hard-packed dirt and mud. It's not so much the difficulty of the climb that will force you to breathe so heavily but rather the paucity of oxygen molecules. Within view of the mountain's peak, an ornate red-and-yellow wooden sign, draped with Buddhist prayer flags, reads:

TAGLANGLA

ALTITUDE: 17,582 FT

YOU ARE PASSING THROUGH SECOND

HIGHEST PASS OF THE WORLD

UNBELIEVABLE IS NOT IT?

Khardung La, just to the north of Leh, claims to be the highest motorable (or bike-able) pass in the world, at more than 5,600 meters, but the designation is disputed. Thus, what is to be believed or unbelieved high in the Himalayas, ultimately, is up to you. The highway between Leh and Manali is maintained by the Indian Army's Border Roads Organization (a.k.a. BRO), and many of BRO's signs offer whimsical and humorous warnings along the oft-treacherous thoroughfare. Along a road where it's not uncommon to see the remnants of a vehicle that tumbled off the cliff, you'll read signs such as I AM CURVACEOUS BE SLOW, and DARLING I LIKE YOU BUT NOT SO FAST.

LEH-MANALI
HIGHWAY

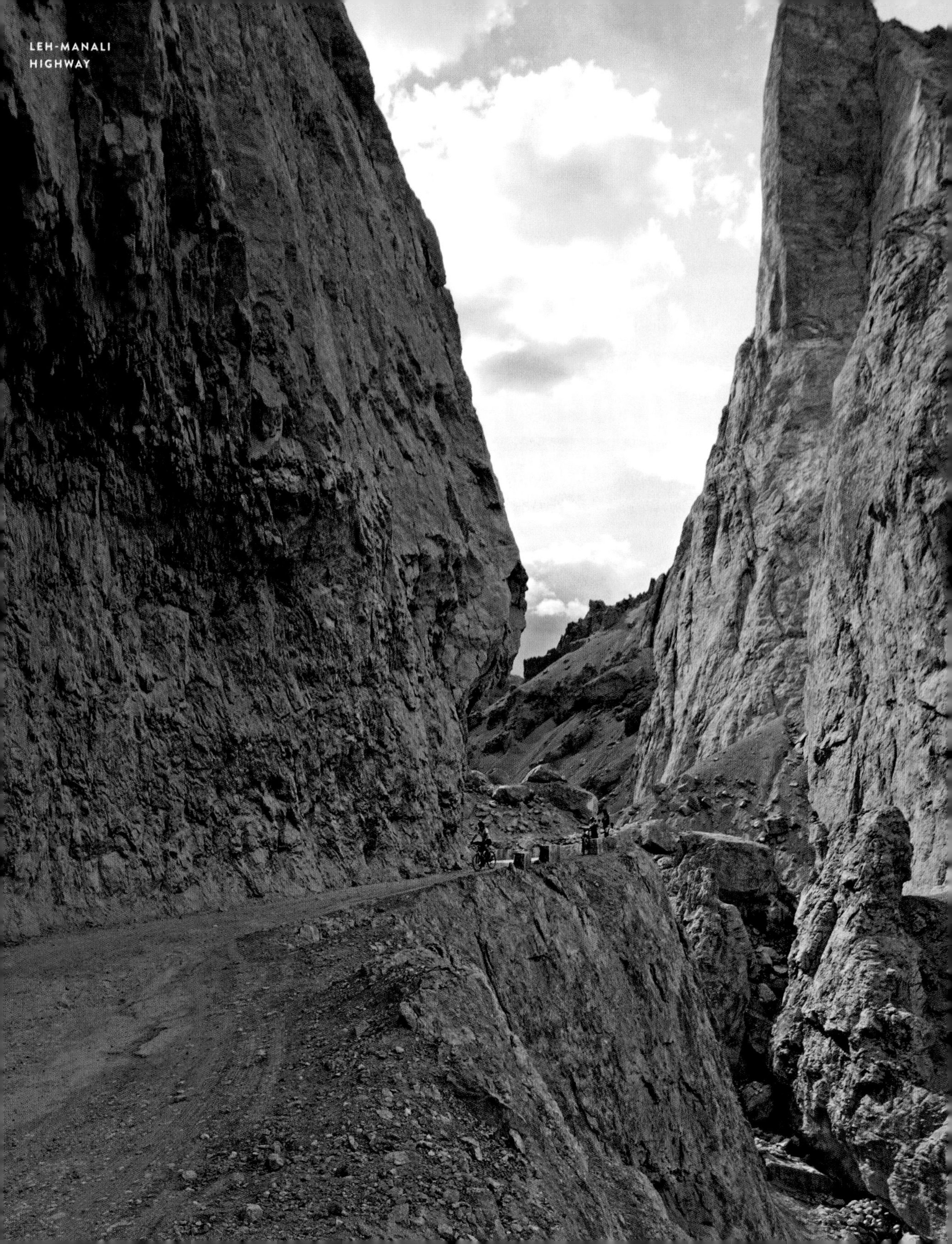

From Taglang La, the Leh–Manali Highway drops into the More Plains, wide open, blustery, and almost utterly free of vegetation, a surreal and haunting landscape reminiscent of a Mars landing. Here, a short detour down a dirt road that is sometimes obscured by the shifting sands leads to an expansive salt lake, the Tso Kar. A salty crust, once mined and exported to Tibet, lines the shore of the emerald-watered lake. Along the lake's freshwater tributaries, green oases of ferns and plants sprout in thick patches. Wild donkeys called *kiang* roam the lake basin, along with Tibetan gazelles, wolves, and foxes. Geese and cranes soar overhead and forage in the grassy marshes.

> **"Along the lake's freshwater tributaries, green oases of ferns and plants sprout in thick patches. Wild donkeys called *kiang* roam the lake basin, along with Tibetan gazelles, wolves, and foxes."**

At the precipitous edge of the More Plains, the road winds down a series of steep curves into the seasonal village of Pang, where fluttering parachute tents offer dormitory-style overnight lodging. Though few humans reside permanently along the Leh–Manali Highway, during the few months of the year when the road is open to traffic, typically from June to October, a number of roadside camps cater to travelers along the route. Though hours may pass without a vehicle or a being along the highway, it's traveled by other car, motorcycle, and bike tourists, as well as colorful Indian trucks, known as *tatas*, which frequently travel in rumbling convoys.

Four more passes loom en route to Manali, each slightly lower in elevation than the next. After summiting the Nakee La pass, the highway descends 700 vertical meters down the Gata Loops, 21 hairpin bends stacked on top of one another like the Alpe d'Huez of the Himalayas. The road follows the sharp edge of the Ling Chu river, brilliant blue with short green grasses and red shrubs bordering its banks. It rolls past stunning rock formations reminiscent of the American Southwest, stone arches and spiral hoodoos towering hundreds of feet overhead. It descends, and descends, and descends, down the Baralacha La pass, through peaks still capped with glistening white snow, through the Lahaul Valley, and then up the final peak, Rhotang La, where the air is thicker and the mountainsides greener.

As the road winds down Rohtang La toward Manali, thick stands of pine trees blanket the slopes and waterfalls pour down rock walls. Civilization, as well, begins to return. Carloads of summer travelers who've never seen snow before frequently drive up the pass to frolic in icy fields, requiring careful and patient navigation on the part of cyclists.

If you come here, know that this is a journey of patience. The Himalayan landscape requires a deliberate pace, as the views prove too immense to hurry and the air is too thin to ride too hard. Most riders take 6 days to complete the trip from Leh to Manali, bringing a tent and overnighting beneath the wide-open Himalayan skies or staying in various pop-up villages along the route, where amenities are close at hand but evenings can provide more ruckus than desired.

The long descent from the Rohtang La pass into Manali brings not only an entirely different landscape but also an entirely different culture. Here, Hindu is the dominant religion, and just outside the small mountain town of Manali is the Hadimba Devi temple, a four-story pagoda situated amidst the tall pines of the Doongri forest. The temple is a popular pilgrimage for tourists, a 2.5-kilometer walk from the nearby tourism office. For those who ride the Leh–Manali Highway, it's a 474-kilometer bike ride from the top of the world.

④

Shiretoko World Heritage Area

JAPAN

On the least-populated, northernmost island of Japan, Hokkaido, a mountainous and remote peninsula extends into the Sea of Okhotsk. The peninsula, said to be the last unexplored area in Japan, is known as Shiretoko, a word derived from the language of the native Ainu, who call this place the end of the earth. Today, it is a national park and UNESCO World Heritage site. The country's densest population of brown bears (a relative of the North American grizzly) and the largest owl in the world, the endangered Blackiston's fish owl, reside in Shiretoko. Hot springs form waterfalls rushing from the rocky mountainsides, and ferry rides offer views of endless cliff faces rising from the completely unspoiled coastline. Those who come to explore this area by bike share their campgrounds with deer and foxes, and they dine on bowls of warm rice topped with raw fish freshly pulled from the sea. They climb the winding Shiretoko pass, crossing the apex of the peninsula at 739 meters, and relax in *onsen*, the pools of naturally heated mineral water. To announce their arrival to the local populace, the bears of Shiretoko, they affix bells to their handlebars, which ring as they ride.

Get There

▸▸ The closest domestic airport to the Shiretoko National Park is Memanbetsu, about 100 kilometers west of the park. Many bike tourists start their adventures in the town of Shari, about 37 kilometers west of the village of Utoro, the latter of which is considered the gateway to the Shiretoko National Park. Numerous outfitters provide supported trips to the park and surrounding areas on the island of Hokkaido. Visit shiretoko.asia for more information.

Sun Moon Lake

If there is a "Made in Taiwan" sticker on one of your bicycles, there is a good chance that it was designed, made, or put together in Taichung City, the capital of the bike industry in Taiwan—and perhaps the world.

The world's largest bicycle manufacturer, Giant, is based in the Taichung City area, as are many other major suppliers that produce the frames and components sold by a variety of international brands. Today, amongst industry insiders, the Taiwanese seal is so sought after that bikes made at a lower cost in China are often brought back to Taiwan for finishing touches, earning them a "Made in Taiwan" sticker.

With the rise of the Taiwanese bike industry, the country has experienced a correlated rise in recreational cycling and now has a flourishing bike culture. The 2006 movie *Island Etude* is often credited with sparking the Taiwanese bike boom. In the film, a young, deaf Taiwanese man partakes in an adventurous circumnavigation of the island, all while carrying a guitar on his back. Following the movie's release, circling Taiwan by bike, a

Get There

▸▸ A popular local training road, Route 136, heads from Taichung City toward Sun Moon Lake. Andrew Kerslake, a cycling writer, also recommends using Routes 147, 68, and 64 to reach the lake via quiet roads that wind through the forested hillsides. Buses between Sun Moon Lake and Taichung City run on a daily schedule, and two bike shops offer rentals, as well as maps of the bike routes around the lake. During the second week of November, Come! Bike Day celebrates cycling at Sun Moon Lake with a number of events, including a mass bike ride around the lake and a vintage bike ride. Visit sunmoonlake.gov.tw/English for more information.

SUN MOON
LAKE

roughly 1,000-kilometer journey, and road riding in general became part of an emerging Taiwanese identity. (Taiwanese nationality is a complex subject. The government of mainland China counts Taiwan as a province, but Taiwan views itself as an independent nation.)

Andrew Kerslake, a cycling writer and cultural critic, who runs the blog *Taiwan in Cycles*, explains that in *Island Etude*, "The romantic image of freedom atop a road bike drew thousands to road cycling, which also appeals to Taiwanese sensibilities in sport. It does not involve physical contact with another competitor, it is not violent or seemingly prone to injury, and it involves some expensive hardware that

> **"Depending on the time of day and the angle of the sun, the waters of Sun Moon Lake vary from translucent shades of topaz to complex deep blues."**

appeals to a prestige society." In 2008, after the CEO of Giant and many other Giant executives completed their own rides around Taiwan, the bike company set up an island-wide bike rental system. Cyclists can pick up a bike at one Giant store and return it at another, making cycling widely accessible to both locals and foreigners. Every weekend in Taichung City, you'll spot hordes of cyclists riding up into the green hills east of the city, many of them headed toward Sun Moon Lake.

One of the most popular tourist destinations in Taiwan, Sun Moon Lake is situated roughly 60 kilometers east of Taichung City, nestled in the foothills of the island's Central Mountains and fed by the rivers and streams flowing from the surrounding peaks. Depending on the time of day and the angle of the sun, the waters of Sun Moon Lake vary from translucent shades of topaz to complex deep blues. Cyclists can take in the splendor of the lake in two ways, via a bike path running along the shoreline or on a serpentine road that forms a 34-kilometer loop around the entirety of the lake. The path, with artful bridges spanning the shimmering inlets and boardwalks alongside the lapping water, provides the most intimate encounter with Sun Moon Lake, while more-experienced cyclists may prefer the open road's undulating terrain and swooping turns.

However, both routes can become crowded with tourists walking, biking, or sightseeing from the double-decker motor coaches that constantly circle the lake. To gain a true appreciation for the riding that surrounds Taichung City and Sun Moon Lake, Kerslake recommends circling the quieter east side of the lake in a clockwise direction from the town of Yuchih. At Ita Thao Village, a left turn leads to Nantou Local Route 63, which ascends into the rural hills overlooking the lake. "The climb is not all that long, but it rises up over the lake with a couple spots for pictures," says Kerslake. Across the summit of the climb, the road follows the contours of the hillside through a Bunun village (one of the indigenous tribes of Taiwan), then launches into a thrilling, serpentine descent that finishes off with a high-speed straightaway. The road ends in a river valley beneath the tall peaks of the Central Mountain Range. On clear days, you can see Yushan, the tallest peak in Taiwan. From here, Highway 16 runs west back toward Taichung City or farther east, winding through the valley and into mountainous rural Taiwan.

Wuling Pass

TAIWAN

On the eastern coast of the island of Taiwan, lush green mountains rise more than 3,000 meters from the shore of the salty sea. The road that cuts across the mountains (of course there's a road) heads north from Hualien, a city of roughly 100,000 inhabitants nestled between the peaks and the Pacific. For 18 kilometers, as it borders the ocean, the route is serene, a flat ride beside the pebble-encrusted beach. Then, where the Liwu River tumbles from the mountains and meets the sea, you cross the expansive steel Tailuge Bridge and veer westward into an immense crevasse, the gaping mouth of the Taroko Gorge.

On its own, riding through the tapered gorge—the sheer walls of marble looming hundreds of feet high on either side, boulders the size of buildings heaped together like mounds of gravel, and white waterfalls streaming down the cliffs—provides an extraordinary sensory experience. Busloads of tourists come here each year to marvel at the gorge and take in the raw power of erosion, its results millions of years in the making. They walk across the Bridge of 100 Lions, lined with white busts of the maned beasts, and through the Tunnel of Nine Turns, a wide trail along the very cusp of the rock face, where the opposing gorge walls sit just 10 meters apart. Adventurous visitors hike the trails high up into the mountainsides and cross the suspension bridges spanning the gorge to achieve incredible views. The solemn pay their respects at the Eternal Spring Shrine, built in honor of the 226 enlisted men who lost their lives during the construction of this road, the Central Cross-Island Highway, which snakes through the Taroko Gorge and continues climbing up and over the crest of Mount Hehuan.

The road through the Taroko Gorge climbs at a gentle gradient of 6 percent, under overhangs and arches cut from the rock wall and across bridges spanning the deep chasm, where the turquoise-tinted river rumbles below. After roughly 18 kilomers (36 kilometers from the seaside city of Hualien), the road ascends from the Taroko Gorge into the surrounding forest. Here, the true challenge begins. The entirety of the ride from Hualien to the summit of the Wuling Pass, a saddle between the two peaks of Mount Hehuan, extends 105 kilometers, rises 3,500 meters in elevation, and is often called the longest (and hardest) mountain climb in the world.

The forest envelopes the road as it winds along the sides of the mountains, only briefly opening up to reveal the green peaks of Taiwan's Central Range spanning the horizon. When you approach the split in the road where the route to the Wuling Pass turns from Highway 8 onto Highway 14, only about 12 kilometers of the 105 total kilometers remain. Yet, according to Kerslake, "The road dishes out enough punishment in the final 12 kilometers to outclass many a queen stage in the Tour de France." As it switchbacks through gnarled juniper trees and across windswept alpine meadows, the road to the Wuling Pass rears up at pitches of more than 20 percent in gradient. Popular with both Taiwanese and foreign cyclists, it's at this point in the climb that you may come across fit-looking riders walking their bikes, overwhelmed by the mountain and the vicious combination of thin air and the abrupt steepness of the road near the summit.

> ## Get There
>
> ▸▸ If simply climbing the Wuling Pass isn't enough, you can sign up for the KOM Challenge, a race held over the same route. In 2012, Danish professional rider and climbing specialist John Ebsen won the inaugural KOM Challenge in 3:37:25. For most experienced cyclists, the climb takes between 5 and 6 hours. There are only a few places to stock up on refreshments along the route, so arrive well stocked with food and water. The Taroko Gorge and nearly the entire climb to the Wuling Pass lie within the boundaries of the Taroko National Park. Visit taroko.gov.tw /English for more information on lodging and transportation near the park.

At the summit, you'll find a large parking lot, a crowded observation deck, and clusters of exhausted cyclists. The main peak of Mount Hehuan, 3,416 meters high, is accessible via a 1-kilometer hike. From there, you can look out across the mountains and the wispy white clouds. You can peer back toward the valley that closes in upon itself, forming the Taroko Gorge, and get a sense of just how far you've come and how high you've climbed.

Australia and
New Zealand

The Forgotten World Highway

There's a reason they call this the Forgotten World. Here in the hilly green heart of New Zealand's North Island, mostly ghosts inhabit the towns, rustic remnants of the rail line that cut across this land a century ago. Sheep, cattle, and the birds soaring overhead are the majority of the companions cyclists have when making the 180-kilometer ride from the village of Taumarunui, where the rail lines converged, to New Plymouth on the country's western coast, a model cycling city (as designated by the New Zealand government).

Officially labeled State Highway 43, the Forgotten World Highway's narrow asphalt lanes and intermittent gravel roads see fewer than 200 vehicles per day, making it one of New Zealand's least-traveled roadways. The ride starts west of Taumarunui, along the banks of the rippling Wanganui River, where the road rises and falls over steep, grassy hills; meanders through lush valleys and thick virgin forests; and slices across deep gorges. Hills that proved too difficult for the road builders to circumvent were punched through to make tunnels that look and feel like caves, water seeping from their stone walls and coarse, rounded ceilings. Locals refer to the constricted, 180-meter-long Moki Tunnel as the hobbit hole.

At roughly the halfway point, the Forgotten World Highway passes through Whangamomona, an independent republic within the nation of New Zealand with a population of 171 people. Here, the historic Whangamomona Hotel, built in 1911, offers travelers of the Forgotten World Highway rest and nourishment, as well as insight into the area's Maori and European history in the abundant photos and memorabilia decorating the walls. From Whangamomona, the cycling route (part of this bike-touring-loving nation's designated network of signed Cycle Trails) turns off the Forgotten World Highway onto Junction Road, an undulating gravel lane with a rugged surface. The road twists and dips through the hills, then returns to pavement after 16 kilometers. At its highest points, where the road rises against the steep cliffsides and the foliage clears, you can catch glimpses of the majestic Mount Egmont, an active volcano rising 2,518 meters above the surrounding farmland. (The mountain is also well known by its Maori name, Mount Taranaki, meaning "shining peak," a reference to its symmetrically snowcapped summit.)

The route gradually descends toward the flat coastal plains and spills out onto the New Plymouth Coastal Walkway, an idyllic 11-kilometer cycling and walking path that borders the Tasman Sea. The path starts at the Taranaki Cycle Park, which features a curvaceous 1.75-kilometer road cycling loop and an outdoor velodrome, then heads south along the shoreline, crossing through lagoons and nature preserves noisy with animal life and past the rumbling waves of sandy surf beaches. When you reach the architecturally acclaimed Te Rewa Rewa bicyclist and pedestrian ridge, a spiral of spikey white ribs that clearly frames Mount Egmont looming in the distance, you've reached the end of the Forgotten World Highway cycling route, and the town of New Plymouth. Here, civilization returns—in perhaps its highest form—with seaside cafes and local art museums to peruse. But the solitude, tranquility, and beauty of the Forgotten World will forever remain a close memory.

Get There

▶▶ Taumarunui, the start of this one-way ride, is a stop on the historic Overlander train (now called the Northern Explorer), which arrives from the major port city of Wellington. Additionally, Taumarunui is serviced by bus from both Wellington and New Plymouth. As New Zealand and municipalities in the Taranaki region work to further develop bicycle tourism, amenities for cyclists along the Forgotten World Highway cycling route are increasing. However, stores where you can restock your food, water, and accommodations for those multiday rides remain sparse and subject to seasonal hours. Call ahead to confirm accommodations, and plan on self-sufficient cycling. Visit nzcycletrail.com for more information.

The Molesworth Muster Trail

Not so long ago, this opulent land, through which one of New Zealand's most treasured cycling trails now passes, was scraped to the bone by overzealous ranchers, transformed into an eroding wasteland, and infested with rabbits. In the late 1800s, Kiwi herders, known as musterers, began driving tens of thousands of sheep and cattle from the port city of Christchurch, on the northeastern coast of New Zealand's South Island, up into this mountainous region known as Molesworth Station. The animals soon grazed away the green shoot grasses that held the thin layer of soil to the hillsides. Hoping to resuscitate the formerly pastoral river valleys by clearing them of inedible vegetation, the hard men who managed the free-roaming herds burned off the remaining tusset grasses, further exacerbating the erosion. Rivers of mud and rock poured down the barren mountain slopes and clogged streambeds. Ranchers nearly eradicated the majestic red deer and hardy mountain goats, which they saw as competition for their domesticated livestock, and threw the entire ecosystem out of balance. European rabbits, erroneously introduced as a game animal in an environment having few predators to control their population, spread like swarms of locusts across Molesworth Station, eating up any surviving grasses. By the mid-1900s, downtrodden ranchers placed the land back in control of the Crown of New Zealand. Rabbit hunters roamed the defunct landscape, filling trenches with poisoned carrots and collecting pelts by the thousands. In 1946, the New Zealand Department of Public Works produced a film titled *A New Zealand Tragedy: The Story of Molesworth*, chronicling the degradation.

The bliss of riding a bike through Molesworth Station today is a testament to the work of the New Zealand Department of Conservation, which now manages the area. A single road, a pathway from the sea first forged by the indigenous Maori, runs through Molesworth Station, taking cyclists on a 207-kilometer journey from Blenheim, on the north coast of the island, down to Hanmer Springs, where thermally heated mineral water wells up from the ground. The challenging but not overly

> **European rabbits spread like swarms of locusts across Molesworth Station, eating up any surviving grasses.**

strenuous ride begins with the gradual 6.5-kilometer climb from Blenheim to the top of Taylor Pass and down a gravel descent to Acheron Road. Here, you'll enjoy a final 16 kilometers or so of asphalt before the sound of gray rocks crunching beneath your wheels accompanies you on the remainder of the journey. Spectacular wildflowers lining the roadsides, fields of green and golden grasses, and the tumbling waters of the Awatere, Acheron, and Clarence Rivers have replaced the bleak scenery that once dominated Molesworth Station. You'll ride through vineyards growing the prized New Zealand sauvignon blanc grapes, over historic suspension bridges with wooden decking, and beneath the 2,000-meter peaks of the Inland Kaikoura Range.

The Molesworth Muster Trail represents a single sliver of the wide web of cycling trails emerging across New Zealand. In 2000, the Otago region of New Zealand, just south of Molesworth Station on the South Island, completed the conversion of an old train line with long viaducts spanning deep river gorges and tunnel entrances faced with century-old stonework into a 150-kilometer-long cycling trail suitable for even novice riders. In 2009, the success of the Otago Rail Trail spurred the New Zealand government to put $50 million toward developing a nationwide network of bike-touring routes and aptly named "Great Rides" showcasing the stunning landscapes, history, and culture of the island nation. Local governments have raised an additional $30 million to add more miles of off-street trails and low-traffic roadways to the network, which is officially called the New Zealand Cycle Trail, or Nga Haerenga ("the journeys") in the Maori language. Today, there are 23 Great Rides across New Zealand's North and South Islands, with communities diligently working to expand and connect the network.

As you pedal the route through Molesworth Station, one of New Zealand's most storied Great Rides, you'll be riding through a working farm, albeit one under much stricter regulation than those of the past. It's not uncommon to encounter a modern-day musterer with a herd of cattle or sheep. The first of the two official campsites in the station arrives at Cob Cottage, 122 kilometers from Blenheim. The historic home here—made from cob, an adobe-like amalgamation of clay, water, gravel, and tusset grasses—was constructed in 1866, and nearby buildings now house the station's farm manager and his family. The Cob Cottage serves as a welcome landmark, and weary cyclists can set up their tents nearby. The second campsite, the Acheron Accommodation House, which dates back to 1863, provided freshly baked bread and a night's rest for travelers driving livestock through the Acheron Valley. From the Acheron Accommodation House campground, a steep 4-kilometer descent drops down Jollies Pass, through thick stands of tall pine trees, and onto the floor of an expansive valley, where you'll arrive in the town of Hanmer Springs.

Get There

▸▸ Due to unpredictable and harsh weather in the highlands of New Zealand, the Molesworth Muster Trail is open to the general public only during the summer, which is from December through April, and with a special access permit from the Department of Conservation during the rest of the year. Many cycling tourists arrive via the Christchurch airport, located 134 kilometers to the south of Hanmer Springs. There's a bicycle assembly station at the Christchurch airport to assist bicycle tourists. A number of touring services offer supported trips on the Molesworth Muster Trail and on New Zealand's other official cycling routes. Visit nzcycletrail.com for more information.

Here, the utter isolation of the Molesworth Station quickly fades and the comforts of civilization return. At an array of quaint pubs and cafes you can get a Kiwi beer or a chilled glass of local white wine, then restore weary and worn body parts at the Hanmer Springs Thermal Pools and Spa.

Victorian Alps

AUSTRALIA

In 1934, after the First World War, as the Great Depression gripped not only the United States but also the entire world, Australia's Dunlop Perdriau tire company organized a 1,000-mile, weeklong bicycle race across Australia with a £1,000 prize. At the time, it was the richest and most prominent bike race ever held in the British Empire, a part of which Australia still remained. Named the Centenary 1000, in honor of the 100-year anniversary of the State of Victoria, the race aspired to mimic the severity of the Tour de France, and the prize money drew top French and Italian racers. The route, as yet untested in a bicycle race, would take on Australia's most fearsome mountains. The Centenary 1000 started in Melbourne on the southern coast with 107 riders toeing the line, then headed east, climbing into the Victorian Alps on rudimentary mountain roads zigzagging across the Australian Highlands.

To split the difference between the two hemispheres' opposing race seasons, the race took place in October—early spring in Australia—and was marred by horrendous weather. A report from the *Gippsland Times* related that "blinding rain storms, howling gales, and morasses of mud had to be fought through by the riders." During one 216-mile stage of the race, riders wobbled along the rocky ledges of Mount Hotham, an alpine giant that rises 1,357 meters over 30 undulating kilometers, kicking above a 10 percent gradient in the final few kilometers before the summit. Just more than half the starters actually completed the inaugural Centenary 1000, an event hampered by weather, crashes amongst the top competitors, and an overly demanding route that made for relatively lethargic racing.

However, the Centenary 1000 did succeed in one respect: It exposed cyclists to

a previously undiscovered frontier for riding. Prior to the event, only hardened gold miners and a handful of sporting trout anglers inhabited this spectacular countryside. Today, the now-paved roads that wind up the exposed ridgelines of Mount Hotham and cut through the deep, brushy valleys of the Victorian Alps—"the bush," as the Aussies call it—constitute some of the most-sought-after cycling terrain in Australia, and the world. The one ride that captures the Alps's most mythic climbs in a single, tantalizingly ambitious loop is known as the three peaks ride, a dawn-to-dusk affair that covers 235 kilometers and climbs 3,856 meters.

After the ascent of Hotham, the three peaks ride gradually descends into the town of Omeo. Situated in the High Plains amidst the surrounding mountain ranges, Omeo served as a pit stop for the Australian stockmen (à la *The Man from Snowy River*) who drove cattle through here in the early 1800s. Cafés and bakeries along the Great Alpine Road in Omeo provide an opportunity to fill up for the two summits ahead. After a brief respite from the up-and-down terrain through the Omeo Valley, the route bends back west into the mountains.

Get There

▶▶ Melbourne, a 4-hour drive southwest of Bright, provides the ideal launch point for an excursion into the Victorian Alps. As a warmup ride, you can spin west from Melbourne on the Great Ocean Road, another quintessential Aussie ride that runs along weather-sharpened ocean cliffsides and topaz blue bays. A number of cycling events are held in the Victorian Alps, with two major rides on the three peaks loop drawing more than 1,000 participants, the Peaks Challenge Falls Creek (bicyclenetwork.com.au/peaks-challenge) and the Audax Alpine Classic (alpineclassic.com.au). Go to visitvictoria.com for more information.

The narrow two-lane road twists and turns along the contours of a deep river gorge, crossing old bridges planked with wooden boards, past signs that warn of kangaroos and wombats crossing, and by the Blue Duck Inn Hotel at Angler's Rest. That establishment, founded during the gold-mining boom, later found it had a more sustainable bonanza in its location at the convergence of three world-class trout streams.

At Bogong High Plains Road, which remained unpaved until 2009, the three peaks route makes a sharp left-hand turn and the pavement rises equally abruptly. The 5 percent average gradient of this rustic road belies its difficulty. From here, it's 23 kilometers to the summit of the climb and 35 kilometers to the resort village of Falls Creek, where the route finally starts descending again. However, it's the first 9 kilometers of the climb to Falls Creek, up to the Raspberry Hill campsite, that leave most riders knock-kneed, with an average gradient of 8 percent and pitches above 15 percent. (Note: Bring low gearing.)

As the road approaches the summit, the wispy stands of trees meld into wide-open plains covered in grasses of green and gray and spotted with rust-red ferns. The route traverses a long plateau until the placid mountain waters of the Rocky Mountain Valley reservoir appear in the distance, denoting a downhill run that drops 1,200 meters over 30 blissful kilometers. The final peak, at least from where we started the three peaks ride, is Towanga Gap, which pales in comparison to the enormity of the ascent to Falls Creek and the climb up Mount Hotham, but at 7.6 kilometers long with a 6.5 percent average gradient, it still presents a considerable obstacle to those clambering up its tree-canopied slopes.

> **Approaching the top of Towanga Gap, there's a clearing in the trees and an overlook with wooden picnic benches. From here, you can look down upon the green farmland of the Kiewa Valley and Mount Bogong, the highest mountain in the Victorian Alps."**

Approaching the top of Towanga Gap, there's a clearing in the trees and an overlook with wooden picnic benches. From here, you can look down upon the green farmland of the Kiewa Valley and Mount Bogong, the highest mountain in the Victorian Alps. You can breathe a sigh of relief that there's just a sloping, downhill descent ahead, culminating in the town of Bright and signaling the completion of the three peaks ride. You can thank the fates that you were born when you were, allowing you the gear ratio and lightweight equipment needed to ease the suffering up the passes of the High Plains, unlike those equally adventurous men who first forged this cycling route through the Alps of Australia nearly a century ago.

Western Tasmania

AUSTRALIA

The ships came down from England, carrying men found guilty of murder and theft, juveniles convicted of poaching and sentenced to hard labor, and political activists accused of inciting protests and sent away for decades. En route to the penal station on Sarah Island, the boats sailed through the narrow, rocky passage of Hells Gate, so-named because of the inhumane conditions awaiting the prisoners on the other side. Escape from this remote end of the world required seizing a vessel and taking to the open sea or cutting across the raw, wild mainland of Tasmania, known as Van Diemen's Land in the 1800s. The odds were against those who ventured into the wilderness. Still, many prisoners dared the escape.

In the 1820s, the convict Alexander Pearce twice disappeared from Sarah Island, once for more than 100 days before being returned to captivity. Immortalized in modern films, Pearce famously survived his treks across the mountainous terrain of western Tasmania by cannibalizing the members of his escape party. Another prisoner, James Goodwin, escaped up the Gordon River on a rudimentary raft made from felled pine trees. Eventually captured a month later, Goodwin's successful navigation of the dense Tasmanian bush led to a rare pardon and his inclusion in a surveying expedition of the previously unexplored land he'd traversed. Other escapees, such as Matthew Brady, became successful bushrangers, bands of robbers who terrorized the colonial government and achieved folk hero status amongst Tasmania's early pioneers.

Today, western Tasmania remains nearly as untamed as it was when those fleeing prisoners first forged across the craggy mountains and forested river valleys.

More than 40 percent of Tasmania is protected parkland, with many of the national and state parks located in the western portion of the island, including the 1.6-million-acre expanse of the Tasmanian Wilderness World Heritage Area. The heart-shaped island of 68,400 square kilometers, roughly the size of West Virginia, is populated by just half a million people, most of whom reside in the capital city of Hobart, on the southern coast. In even more sparsely populated western Tasmania, you're as likely to come across the screeching, bared-teethed growl of a Tasmanian devil or the fascinating animal amalgam the duck-billed platypus as you are to run into another vehicle on the road. Riding a bike through this western portion of Tasmania—through ancient rain forests, around glacial lakes, and beneath jagged mountain peaks—is to traverse some of the last true wilderness on earth.

Circumnavigate western Tasmania by starting in the historic mining outpost of Queenstown, the west coast's largest city. Situated deep in the Queen River Valley, Queenstown served as the center of a booming mining business, with deep veins of gold and copper running through nearby Mount Lyell. In its heyday, the hillsides surrounding Queenstown were stripped for lumber, leading to erosion (the area gets 2.5 meters of rain per year) that washed away the topsoil and left behind an eerie, barren landscape of open rock faces hued in pink and gold. Today, the inhabitants of Queenstown subsist on the vestiges of copper remaining deep within Mount Lyell, as well as on the recent influx of tourists who come to ride the restored West Coast Wilderness Railway, constructed in 1894 to export ore from Queenstown to the port at Strahan.

Get There

▸▸ Daniel Strauss, the co-owner of Soigneur (soigneur.cc), which specializes in fully supported bespoke cycling trips, suggests the route described here. In 2012, Strauss made his own exploration of the Tasmanian wilderness while participating in the Rapha Continental Van Dieman's Land ride. The loop described in this chapter, 240 kilometers long, is best completed in 2 days but can be ridden in 1 day by the truly hardcore. Visit westernwilderness.com.au for more information on lodging and local amenities.

From Queenstown, the Lyell Highway parallels the Wilderness Railway for 40 kilometers through dense forest preserves before arriving in Strahan, situated on the Macquarie Harbor. A quick boat ride from Strahan will deliver you to Sarah

Island, where the ominous redbrick ruins of the penal station remain. A popular tourism outpost, Strahan is considered the gateway to the Franklin-Gordon Wild Rivers National Park and is also situated at the southern terminus of 15 kilometers of pristine coastline known as Ocean Beach.

From Strahan, the route heads north on Zeehan-Strahan Road, across the Henty River on a wooden bridge and beneath low-slung alpine mountains, the harbingers of a series of climbs to come. Zeehan, 45 kilometers north of Strahan, offers one of the last true townships at which to refuel before submerging yourself deeper into the wilds of western Tasmania. As you ride north from Zeehan toward the placid waters of Lake Pieman, the narrow two-lane road winds along the lower slopes of Mount Livingstone, never taking on an extended ascent but rather going ever up and down. The easterly road through this region, known as the Tarkine wilderness, was primarily built for the construction of the hydroelectric Reece Dam and has seen little traffic since the project's completion in 1987. The dam, though stunning with its overlook of the rolling green hills and the rain forest of beech and myrtle trees, is indicative of Tasmania's ongoing environmental debate. Though the Australian state prides itself on the wild, unspoiled nature of its protected lands, it also faces a constant struggle over how to best utilize its natural resources, primarily the damming and mining of its western rivers and mountains. A large contingent of Tasmanians hopes to forever protect the Tarkine by adding it to the Tasmania Wilderness World Heritage Area while others aim to harvest the vast mineral deposits hidden beneath the soil.

Approaching the village of Tullah, 100 kilometers from Zeehan, the imposing stone turrets of Mount Murchison, western Tasmania's tallest peak at 1,275 meters, appear in the distance. The pass across Mount Murchison represents the longest ascent on the route, rising 457 meters in 16 kilometers. As the road descends back toward Queenstown, it passes through the heart of the officially designated Tasmanian Wilderness World Heritage Area. Intermittent stretches of smooth gravel border marshes and meadows bursting with plant and animal life and placid lakes and jagged mountains steeping in low-lying mist. Amidst this landscape, there's nothing but the monotonous crunching of earth beneath your tires, the fragrant breezes blowing across the valleys, the racing beat of your own heart being sped up by your exertion, and the exhilaration you feel.

Central America
and the Caribbean

LA RUTA DE LOS CONQUISTADORS, COSTA RICA

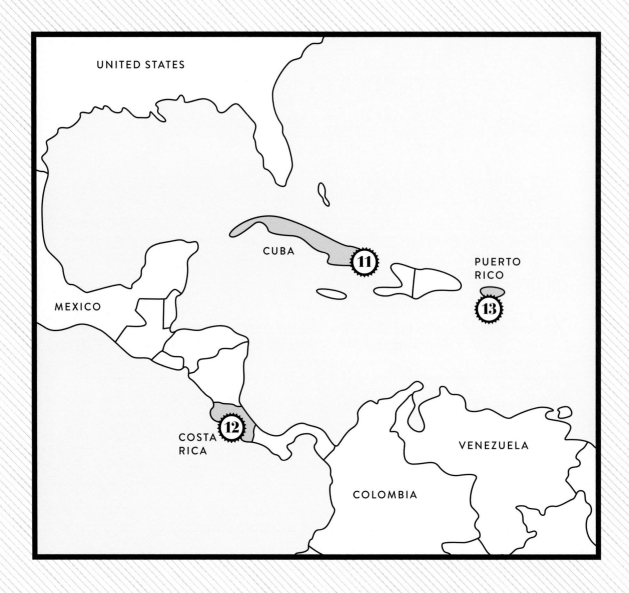

Loma de la Farola

CUBA

Christopher Columbus landed here, in Baracoa, in 1492. In his diary, he described the topaz blue bay and tropical foliage–laden hills as "the most beautiful place in the world." Subsequent Spanish explorers christened Baracoa Cuba's first capital city in 1511, but by the mid-16th century, conflict with the indigenous Taíno and roaming pirates had left the remote colony nearly abandoned. Then, in 1964, the newly formed Castro regime completed a serpentine mountain road, La Farola, linking the windy and dry southern coast near Guantanamo Bay with the verdant north, giving the former capital city new life. The impressive feat of road construction, with 11 bridge crossings, traverses 55 kilometers from coast to coast and rises 600 meters above the surrounding sea. The road is regularly used in the Vuelta Ciclística a Cuba, the national bike race that also dates back to 1964, and with good reason.

> ### Get There
>
> ▸▸ While at the time of publication tourist travel to Cuba is still prohibited for US citizens and others under US jurisdiction, according to the US Department of State, this prohibition is expected to be lifted in the near future. For non-US citizens, Cuba is one of the most popular tourist destinations in the Caribbean. Visit baracoa.org for more information.

From Baracoa, La Farola runs through a shallow valley before starting an undulating climb to the crest of the mountain chain. The two-lane road frequently cantilevers away from the mountainsides, carving across rock faces and providing sweeping views of the mountainous jungle, a wrinkled sheet of lush peaks and ridgelines disappearing into the steamy horizon. At the top of La Farola,

35 kilometers from Baracoa, a small outpost offers refreshments found only in this part of the country. The *cucurucho* is Cuba's version of an organic energy bar, a paste made from shredded coconut, honey, sugar, and various fruits and nuts, then wrapped in a palm leaf.

From its peak, La Farola plunges back toward the sea over 20 kilometers of steep descents and intermittent uphills. Where the road flattens and bends to the west, the Caribbean Sea emerges. Rocky bluffs front the shore, and cacti grow in the arid climate here on the island's southern coast.

> **In his diary, Christopher Columbus described the topaz blue bay and tropical foliage–laden hills as 'the most beautiful place in the world.'**

For modern adventurers, Cuba retains much of the beguiling nature that Columbus documented upon landing on the shore in Baracoa. On La Farola, you'll see locals traveling on horseback and pedaling homemade cargo bikes, but as a result of the long-standing US trade embargo, you'll encounter little auto traffic. For cyclists, that makes the ride from Baracoa one of the most beautiful in the world.

La Ruta de Los Conquistadores

COSTA RICA

Simply known as *La Ruta* to those who've come here and conquered, this 3-day mountain bike stage race crosses Costa Rica from the Pacific to the Caribbean coast, covering 280 kilometers and climbing more than 6,600 meters. The race follows a path cut by Spanish conquistadors across the dense jungle and volcanic mountains of this incredibly biologically diverse country, which contains 5 percent of the world's flora and fauna within only 1/100th of the planet's land mass. You'll climb the rocky slopes of the Irazú Volcano, topping out at more than 3,000 meters above sea level, and spend equally as much time coming down a descent so long and steep you'll need new brake pads by the time you reach the bottom. You'll hike across train trestles above roaring rivers and finish on a sandy beach, racing alongside the Caribbean Sea. La Ruta de Los Conquistadores claims to be the first mountain bike stage race in the world, and it certainly remains one of the hardest. It took those original explorers 20 years to make their way across this rugged country. For most competitors at La Ruta, simply finishing is a victory.

> ## Get There
>
> ▶▶ An all-inclusive international racer package covers lodging, food, and transportation during La Ruta for $1,700. Visit adventurerace.com for more information.

La Vuelta Puerto Rico

With their lights blinking in the still-dark early morning, every January, 500-plus avid road cyclists roll out across the cobblestone streets of Old San Juan, the colonial heart of Puerto Rico. Over 3 days, the riders make a 600-kilometer circumnavigation of the entire island. They pedal beneath canopies of palm trees, along the Atlantic coast, and over terrain that varies from windswept flats to rolling hills and punishingly steep climbs. And they complete the entire ride as a group, led by road captains who help maintain a consistent pace.

La Vuelta Puerto Rico is an event unlike any other. The distances are demanding, with days of 250, 130, and 210 kilometers. The scenery is surreal, with views of the sandy coast to one side and the mountainous interior of the island to the other. The ride's support caters to every need. At the start of each day, a slow-paced neutral rollout stops at a breakfast buffet of eggs, pancakes, and *avena,* a Puerto Rican oatmeal made with cinnamon and vanilla. Every 32 kilometers or so the groups arrive at fully stocked rest stops that often feature live music and dancing, and friendly volunteers offer bags of ice to combat the sometimes sweltering humidity.

Get There

▶▶ Registration for La Vuelta Puerto Rico opens in April and ranges from $450 to $700, depending on how early you sign up and if and when it sells out. The registration fee includes daily breakfasts and lunches and dinner at the ride's closing ceremony, as well as a custom La Vuelta Puerto Rico jersey. Though lodging is not included, the organizers arrange with various hotels in each city for the transport of rider luggage. Visit vueltapr.com for more information.

Sag wagons offer lifts to riders who break down, and mechanics wrench riders' bikes in return for tips. But what truly sets La Vuelta Puerto Rico apart is its packs, pelotons of A, B, and C riders, dictated by average speeds that range from hammerheads doing 40 kilometers per hour to recreational cyclists riding between 25 and 30 kilometers per hour, with each group determined to roll across the finish line each day en masse. The opportunity to take on such a physically daunting tour while being sucked along by a steadily moving draft is one of the main reasons the ride draws more than half of its participants from as many as 35 different countries.

The long days in the saddle don't leave lots of energy for exploring, but riders of La Vuelta Puerto Rico still find time to relax on the beach, sipping from freshly cut coconuts while watching the sun set over the western coast. They suck down drinks spiked with rum and go salsa dancing after the finish in Old San Juan. Then they leave Puerto Rico and go home and tell their friends, "You must come ride here."

"They pedal beneath canopies of palm trees, along the Atlantic coast, and over terrain that varies from windswept flats to rolling hills and punishingly steep climbs."

Europe

MAJORCA, SPAIN

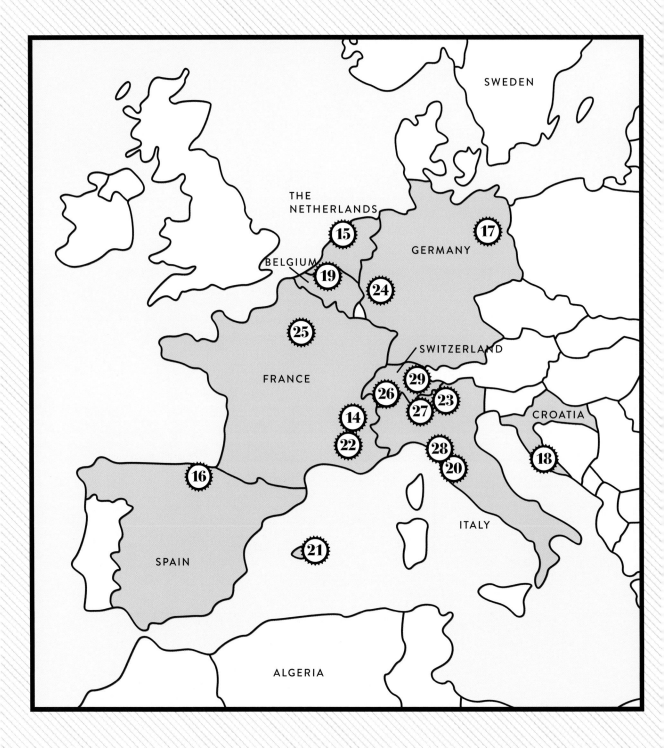

(14)

Alpe d'Huez

FRANCE

"**S**o much happens before the cameras turn on and the fans tune in," professional cyclist Tejay van Garderen says, recalling his dramatic role in a historic race on the mountain seemingly synonymous with the Tour de France. In 2013, van Garderen was leading Stage 18 of the Tour, just over a kilometer from the summit finish atop Alpe d'Huez. When those who witnessed the race think back to those final few kilometers (including van Garderen himself), they most vividly remember van Garderen's legs going weak and wobbly on the steep final pitch, with the Frenchman Christophe Riblon hunting him like crippled prey.

But, as van Garderen points out, a FINISH banner doesn't just represent the sum of the kilometers that led to the line. Behind every finish line is a longer story, one that's rarely told as the action unfolds or detailed in post-race recaps. To understand the emotions that ran through van Garderen as he stood and struggled to pedal up that final pitch, you must also understand Alpe d'Huez—called simply the Alpe—and why this mountain, in a sport full of mountains, rises above all others.

Van Garderen, who'd previously finished fifth overall in the Tour de France, entered the 2013 Tour de France aiming for a podium position. Only because he'd failed to meet his own expectations in the 17 exhausting days of racing prior to the Alpe d'Huez stage was he given the opportunity to vie for the stage win. As the 2013 Tour de France, the much celebrated 100th running of the race, wound toward the high peaks of the Alps, van Garderen sat in 50th place overall, more than an hour behind the overall race leader, British racer Chris Froome.

Van Garderen knew that if he won on Alpe d'Huez, he would not only salvage his disappointing tour but also secure a career-defining victory and write his name into the history of the mountain. (Literally—the name of at least one of the Alpe's 28 winners is engraved on a plaque at each of the 21 bends leading to the peak.) But targeting victory atop the mountain is one thing, actually arriving first quite another. Everyone wants to win on Alpe d'Huez. And in 2013, winning on the Alpe would prove harder than any year prior. In a sadistic celebration of the centennial tour, the organizers had designed a route concluding with not just one, but two trips up the Alpe. In 2013, the climb's 21 tight switchbacks would total 42. Instead of the traditional 13-kilometer race to the summit at an average gradient of 7.6 percent, van Garderen and his pursuers would ascend more than 25 kilometers on the Alpe. In order to run the tour up the Alpe two times consecutively, tour organizers unveiled an entirely new road in the Tour de France, the Col de Sarenne, which descends down the sheer glacial plane on the mountain's leeward side. Riders howled in protest at the dangerous, bumpy descent—van Garderen called it a goat path—but the tour, as it'd done 99 times before, would race on.

One thing you frequently hear about the Alpe is that it is not Europe's most difficult climb, nor even its most scenic. (The second assertion is undoubtedly contested by the inhabitants of the Romanche River valley, from which the Alpe rises. Locals refer to the mountain as the Island of the Sun in tribute to the 300-plus days of sunshine the south-facing slope receives annually.) It's true, a number of taller, longer, and perhaps more difficult climbs—the Galibier, Ventoux, and Tourmalet—have earned firm positions in the lore of the Tour de France. Mountains in Spain and Italy—respectively, the Alto del Angliru and Mount Zoncolan—feature ramps above 20 percent in gradient and bring the world's best cyclists to a near standstill on their impossible steep slopes. Yet, it is the Alpe, and the Alpe

Get There

▸▸ Alpe d'Huez, home to some of France's best ski runs, is best known as a cycling destination. Bike shops, bars, hotels, and restaurants in both Bourg d'Oisans, the town at the base of the mountain, and the resort atop Alpe d'Huez cater to the cycling set. To pay homage to the man who first promoted the Tour de France stage, Georges Rajon, book a room at the Hotel Le Christina, where many famous Tour de France riders have slept. The closest airport is in Grenoble. Visit the mountain's official tourism site, alpedhuez.com, for more information.

alone, that inspires more devotion amongst the followers of the Tour de France than any other mountain pass. Almost every year (the tour rarely bypasses the Alpe), hundreds of thousands of fans migrate to the serpentine road, parking recreational vehicles and erecting campgrounds as much as a week in advance of the race's arrival. The road turns into the world's grandest stadium carved into a mountainside. On days the tour doesn't visit the Alpe, it remains a mecca for bicyclists. During the summer, as many as 1,000 cyclists a day flock to the mountain. The local tourism bureau issues official time cards, allowing riders to punch in their start times at the bottom of the mountain and record their own records at the top.

The story of the Alpe as a magnet for cycling enthusiasts begins in the winter of 1952, with an industrious Frenchman named Georges Rajon who owned a hotel at the ski resort atop Alpe d'Huez. At the time, recreational skiing had yet to achieve widespread popularity, and Rajon, an ardent promoter of the resort as well as an avid sportsman, sought to increase the national profile of the mountain. In the Tour de France, which had captivated the nation for nearly half a century, Rajon saw the perfect marketing vehicle for the Alpe. A well-known artist, Jean Barbaglia, lived in the town at the foot of the Alpe, Bourg d'Oisans and happened to be a close friend of the tour's route director. Through Barbaglia, Rajon convinced the organizers of the tour to come preview the mountain. When they agreed, he rallied patrons in the community to pay the fee associated with hosting a stage. On July 4th of 1952, the Tour would race up the Alpe and finish at the top. It would be the first time a tour stage would finish on the summit of a mountain. And, perhaps even more revolutionary for the event, the race would be broadcast to television viewers from cameras on motorbikes. Rajon would serve as an official scorer, anxiously waiting at the top to mark down the finishers' names on a large chalkboard.

However, in an era without featherlight carbon fiber bikes, when racers rode massive gears and carried spare tires draped across their shoulders, the first mountaintop finish proved too ominous for the pack of riders. Exhausted from 10 arduous days of racing prior to the Alpe, they rode the entirety of the 265-kilometer route preceding the final climb at a leisurely pace and fell as much as 40 minutes behind the predicted finish time. Once up and onto the Alpe's 21 switchbacks for the first time, the Italian campionissimo, Fausto Coppi, easily dispatched his rivals and donned the yellow jersey on the podium. After the stage, Coppi openly wondered why his rivals hadn't attacked. Whom had they feared more, him or the mountain?

The tour's first summit finish, won by the sport's biggest star and broadcast on television for the first time, should have proved a resounding success. But after the stage, Alpe d'Huez drew more criticism than applause. Journalists complained that the demanding 265-kilometer stage had been reduced to nothing more than a 13-kilometer slog. Even the tour's chief, Jacques Goddet, conceded that the first run up the Alpe had lacked theatrics, and declined to press for more mountaintop finishes in future tours. The race wouldn't return to the Alpe for another 24 years.

As he warmed up on a stationary trainer prior to the start of Stage 18 during the 2013 Tour, Tejay van Garderen wasn't thinking about the sordid early history of the Alpe. Rather, he was focused on preparing for his own double assault on the climb, 61 years after the tour had first gone up the mountain. The 172-kilometer stage would begin at the base of the Col de Manse, a relatively short but still difficult pass, and van Garderen anticipated a feverish start. Rival teams had been relentlessly attacking the yellow-jersey wearer, Chris Froome, early and often in the mountains, and all of the tour's top climbers would battle to make the day's early breakaway. As predicted, moments after the racers rolled off the line and headed up the Col de Manse, the peloton imploded. But van Garderen succeeded in making the breakaway group of nine riders. He drove the pace alongside his fellow escapees as they crested two more mountain passes, the Rampe du Motty and Col d'Ornan, en route to the Alpe. Entering the town of Bourg d'Oisans 108 kilometers into the race, at the foot of the first ascent of the Alpe, his group held an 8-minute advantage on the chasing field.

While 8 minutes may seem like a large gap, with 65 kilometers still to race, two ascents of the Alpe before him, and an attacking field behind, van Garderen doubted he'd stay away. "I figured the advantage would get cut in half by the time we reached the top," van Garderen said. He decided that if winning wasn't a likely possibility, he'd at least put on a show. The steep initial pitches of Alpe d'Huez come as a stark introduction to the mountain, and most riders who've ascended it will tell you that the first kilometer feels the hardest. Here, van Garderen looked at the faces of the riders surrounding him, saw agony, and accelerated. The Frenchman, Riblon, and a young Italian, Moreno Moser, stuck with him, but soon van Garderen shed them, too.

The higher van Garderen ascended, the thicker the crush of spectators became—a sea of people, suddenly parting before him. The mountain face was so sheer, the road up it so circuitous, that fans eagerly awaiting the arrival of the leader on the Alpe leaned over the cliffside's stone retaining walls and peered down to see van Garderen pedaling through the turns below. As van Garderen rode toward the clouds, he could count the turns to the top, numbered in descending order . . . 17 . . . 14 . . . 11. At turn 7, the Dutch Corner, he neared the heart of the insanity of Alpe d'Huez. It was the Dutch, even more so than the French, who helped transform the Alpe into the mythic climb it is today by winning 8 of the first 14 finishes up the mountain and subsequently claiming the entire Alpe as a territory of Holland. The Dutch Corner is the epicenter of the nation's adulation for the Alpe, attracting thousands of fans, and van Garderen knew the reception might be special. He is of Dutch heritage and had spent the early part of his professional career living with an aunt and uncle in Holland and racing for a Dutch team. When he looked up the road ahead, he saw a sea of orange, spectators clad head to toe in the national color. He could hear them chanting his name.

In 1976, the Alpe got its second chance after a scheduled tour stage in nearby Grenoble fell through. In the 24 years since the tour's last visit to the Alpe, summit finishes had become de rigueur for modern bike races. The less conventional organizers of the Giro d'Italia and the Vuelta a España, the national tours of Italy and Spain that are constantly trying to one-up each other, had sought out the steepest pitches to end their most demanding mountain stages on. Eventually, the tour followed suit. When a journalist and friend of hotel owner Georges Rajon suggested to the tour's route director that Alpe d'Huez replace the canceled Grenoble stage, the anticlimactic finish of the tour's first visit to the Alpe seemed like a distant memory. The route director agreed, and Rajon secured the funds to host the stage. The racers would make another assault on Huez.

As if he had known the world's biggest bike race would once again return to the Alpe, in 1964 Rajon had led the installation of the numbered hairpin turns that would further cement the Alpe's legend. Rajon took the idea from the Vršič Pass in Slovenia, a behemoth of a mountain in the Julian Alps that bears a marker at each of its 53 turns. Rather than count up, as the Vršič does, Rajon decided that the Alpes' turns should count down, so riders knew just how many switchbacks remained. The plaques marking the numbered switchbacks also note their altitudes, as well as the altitude of the town of Huez (below the resort, at 1,448 meters), the altitude of the race's finish at the resort (1,860 meters), and the altitude of the mountain peak (3,330 meters). Thanks to Rajon's signs, riders on the Alpe always know how high they've climbed, and how many more meters remain.

Dutchman Joop Zoetemelk won a sprint finish atop the Alpe in the tour's return, while the Belgian Lucien Van Impe took an esteemed consolation prize atop the Alpe, the yellow jersey, and eventually the overall title at the '76 Tour de France.

During the ensuing years, 11 riders in total would secure the tour's overall victory on the Alpe by either donning the yellow jersey or further increasing their overall lead. Every time a racer claimed yellow or cemented a victory atop the Alpe, the mountain further ingrained itself in the history of the tour.

Though no Dutch rider has won a stage atop the Alpe since 1989, the nation's adulation endures. At turn seven, the road up Alpe d'Huez is a scant 2.5 lanes wide, yet somehow an entire Dutch village blossoms in the days leading up to the tour's arrival. Camper buses crowd the edges of the roadside, air mattresses are inflated beneath makeshift tents, generators power televisions broadcasting the race and building anticipation before the competitors' arrival, and long lines of hungry, thirsty fans form outside the ever-entrepreneurial vendors selling beer and frites. Those without a sliver of the mountain on which to rest their heads simply don't sleep. The pre-party for a race that passes by in mere moments lasts throughout the day and the night. Traditional Dutch anthems and European pop songs blare. People clad in all manner of costumes (some wearing nothing, or very close to nothing at all) dance in the road throughout the night.

Between the two parting rows of spectators the road narrowed to shoulder's width as van Garderen entered the Dutch Corner. His lungs heaved, and with each breath, he brought in the malty scent of cheap beer, gallons of which had been consumed prior to his arrival. It splashed from the cups of fans as they leaned into the lenses of the cameras following the race, and it glistened where it'd been spilled onto the bright orange paint covering the entire width of the corner. Riblon followed close behind, ducking beneath flags whose holders had failed to clear them from his path, and Moser was close behind him. At the summit of the first trip up the Alpe, van Garderen was told the gap back to the field of overall contenders behind remained a gaping 7 minutes. He'd succeeded in putting on a show, but now he realized he could win on the Alpe and was kicking himself for having wasted too much energy early in the stage. Knowing he might need their help later, van Garderen waited for Riblon and Moser to rejoin him. With another trip up the Alpe awaiting them, the three riders began the ominous descent of the Col de Sarenne.

"Between the two parting rows of spectators the road narrowed to shoulder's width."

By European standards, the road up Alpe d'Huez, 28 feet across at its widest section, is a veritable highway. The width, in part, is what allows for the massive congregation of fans, who bring with them camper buses and tents and various other forms of infrastructure that a narrower mountain road would not permit. In comparison, the road down the Sarenne measures barely an automobile's width. There were no stone barricades in the corners to guard riders and vehicles from slipping over the edge. A litany of cracks and bumps marred the Sarenne's concrete surface. In the 2013 Tour de France, organizers allowed the race's television motorcycles to film the racers only from behind and prohibited spectators from congregating on the Sarenne. There simply wasn't enough room for them and the race at one time. But the organizers' inclusion of the Sarenne in the centennial running of the tour may not have only been done to make a double ascent of the Alpe possible. Many speculated that the nearby communities hoped to showcase the alternative route down the Alpe to the thousands of amateurs who visit the climb each year. If even a fraction of them chose to include the Sarenne in their routes, it would help ease some of the congestion on the road during the peak tourism months.

For van Garderen, the concerns over the Sarenne's rough surface unfortunately came to fruition. In a bumpy corner, his bike's chain jumped off the cassette and lodged between the frame and the gear cluster. Unable to pedal, he waited on his team car, following close behind, for a new bike. By the time he'd remounted, he'd lost nearly 50 seconds to Riblon and Moser. He would need to embrace gravity—in its most terrifying form, rocketing downhill on the 21-kilometer-long descent—in order to catch the leader before the final climb of the Alpe.

A platitude you often hear when a racecourse appears easy, too flat, or too short to truly challenge the best riders in the world is that the racers make the race, not the route. If the racers choose to race in an attacking style, the race will prove difficult and exciting. But the opposite is true, as well. In the instances when promoters have sought the steepest and highest mountains or lengthened routes beyond our traditional conceptions of human endurance, the actual racing frequently fails to impress. Riders arrive at the finish exhausted, unable to produce the sharp accelerations and down-to-the-wire battles that captivate audiences. This occurred on the tour's first visit to the Alpe, in 1952. When the racers arrived, they'd been on their saddles for 8 hours. It's no wonder that the action on the Alpe produced a negative reaction from the tour's critics. But since the tour's return to the mountain, many of cycling's most legendary battles, a number of them including Americans, have been waged on the climb's 21 tight switchbacks.

As the reign of the Dutch riders wound to a close in the late '80s, a young American rose to prominence at the tour. Though he never won atop the Alpe, Greg LeMond cemented two of his three Tour de France victories on the mountain. In '86, LeMond crossed the finish line hand in hand with his teammate, the Frenchman Bernard Hinault, and in '90, en route to his third overall Tour de France victory, he narrowly lost a sprint finish to Italian racer Gianni Bugno. In 1992, another American, the lithe climber Andy Hampsten, raced to victory on the Alpe. Like van Garderen, Hampsten inserted himself into an early breakaway, then set a hard pace at the bottom and made it harder as he reached the top. Hampsten called his ride on the Alpe "my best win," and said, "I wouldn't trade this for a world championship." The last American to win on the Alpe no longer officially remains in the record books. Lance Armstrong won on Alpe d'Huez twice, in 2001 and during a time trial up the mountain in 2004. Armstrong's 2001 victory is known, simply, as "the look." He spent the early part of the race toward the Alpe at the back of the field, feigning fatigue. However, once up and onto the mountain, Armstrong peered into the eyes of his main rival, the big German Jan Ullrich, then rode away, alone.

When he was growing up in Bozeman, Montana, van Garderen knew the Alpe d'Huez was special, that it carried extra significance, because he was the son of a bike racer. He understood that if there was one day in the tour to watch, one mountain to climb yourself, it was the Alpe. But as a professional racer focused on performing well in the overall classification, not individual victories, he viewed the Alpe as just another climb, a place to make or lose time against his rivals. It wasn't until the 2013 Tour de France, when he circled the stage in his race bible and dug deep to make the day's breakaway, that he found himself alone, out in front on the tour's most iconic climb, that the Alpe suddenly meant everything. He knew the racers who'd won atop the Alpe had written themselves into the history of the Tour de France, and he wouldn't give up his chance to join them. By the bottom of the Sarenne, he'd rejoined the leading duo, Riblon and Moser. Minutes later, the three riders turned right off the valley road and headed back up the Alpe. Riblon was the first to attack. He stood on the pedals and in a flurry of circles rode away from Moser. Van Garderen marked him immediately, and from these two men, a winner would emerge. Behind them, the peloton chased rabidly. A 7-minute gap could easily evaporate on the 13 kilometers up the Alpe.

As Riblon and van Garderen rounded turn 20, van Garderen rose from the saddle and accelerated. Riblon grimaced. As the two riders entered turn 19, the road flattened momentarily, and as they exited, it steepened. Again, van Garderen attacked. Twelve kilometers from the summit of Alpe d'Huez, he was alone at the head of the race. Later, van Garderen said that maybe he should have waited to attack Riblon, worked with him, used him, then tried to shed him near the top of the mountain. But Riblon had just attacked, and the opportunity to counter was fleeting. As a racer primarily focused on the overall classification, van Garderen felt somewhat out of his element in focusing solely on the stage win. It didn't matter how much time he gained or lost on the day, only whether he won or not. He quickly put 30 seconds between himself and Riblon and still held 4 minutes on the yellow jersey that was chasing him. More than once, an overzealous fan leapt from the crowd and ran beside van Garderen. More than once van Garderen reached out and shoved the fan aside, momentarily breaking his concentration, his rhythm. ("The spectators are incredible, except when they run," says van Garderen. "Don't run.") At the halfway point of the mountain, he again entered the Dutch Corner, and he again heard them screaming his name. A man, entirely naked except for a lime-green Speedo, the sides of which were stretched over his shoulders rather than around his waist, stood beside the road and roared, beating his chest like a gorilla.

At just under 3.5 kilometers from the summit of the Alpe, the barriers appeared, pushing back the fans, giving van Garderen the full width of the road. But without the energy of the encroaching crowd, his cadence seemed to slow, his shoulders rocked. "I felt the lights turning off," says van Garderen. For the first time since leaving Riblon near the base of the Alpe, he tilted his head and looked back over his right shoulder. He saw the Frenchman gaining. Just over 1.5 kilometers from the summit of the Alpe, the road pitched up, the last segment of steepness before a gradual run into the resort and the FINISH banner. Here, van Garderen lost the race. Riblon caught him, and surged past him. Van Garderen, exhausted, couldn't respond. The Frenchman celebrated his biggest victory, only the third time the home nation had won atop the Alpe. As he pedaled the kilometer, van Garderen's face betrayed defeat.

Of the dozens of Tour de France stages held at Alpe d'Huez, the stage on which the racers summited the climb twice will undoubtedly remain one of its most memorable. Perhaps, decades from now, van Garderen will look back on the race and take some solace in the fact that he rode heroically on one of the Tour de France's most legendary days. The kind of dramatic racing van Garderen's performance on the Alpe demonstrated, racing for the win, his eyes resolute, his pedal stroke smooth and sure, is exactly why so many people travel to this mountain. Why they wait by the roadside for hours to catch a glimpse of the courage the racers display as they battle the 21 switchback turns, and one another. Why they pedal up it themselves, envisioning a crowd parting before them, a pursuer hunting them down, a celebration at the summit.

Van Garderen was 25 years old the day of his historic ride on Alpe d'Huez. Perhaps in 10 years, or 20, or 40 years, when he thinks about the day he raced up the mountain two times consecutively, maybe he will no longer feel the sting of defeat but take pride in his historic ride on one of the Tour de France's most historic days. His name may not appear on a plaque, marking one of the 21 switchbacks, but he certainly wrote himself into the history of the race. Does that not offer any solace? No, says van Garderen. On that day, the mountain became too important, a victory at the top too meaningful. He finds no consolation in the beauty of his struggle, the passion of the fans, the immensity of the Alpe. "I will always see it as a missed opportunity," he says, "as the biggest disappointment of my career."

Amsterdam

THE NETHERLANDS

The beauty of the world's bike commuting epicenter—where 60 percent of urban trips occur by bike, on separated pathways with cycling-specific traffic signals—is that most Dutch don't cycle specifically to lose weight or make an environmental statement. They ride because cycling is the city's quickest, most convenient, and safest form of transportation. They ride because it's just . . . normal. Here, bikes rule. But it wasn't always this way.

Following World War II, cars came to dominate Dutch transportation. City plazas turned into parking lots, and wrecking balls knocked down brick buildings to widen roads for automobiles. Planners even discussed filling Amsterdam's iconic canals with concrete to increase car capacity. Like much of the rest of the developed world, the Netherlands became infatuated with cars and the individual mobility they promised. But by the 1970s, the love affair had turned sour. Traffic jammed the narrow roads of historic Dutch cities, the nation was held hostage by a foreign oil crisis, and its citizens

Get There

▶▶ Bike rentals and guided cycling tours are available throughout Amsterdam. As cycling is integrated into everyday life, most Dutch bike commuters (which is most Dutch people) don't wear specific cycling clothes or helmets. However, a good lock is an essential piece of equipment. Visit bikingamsterdam.com for a comprehensive list of suggested cycling routes just outside the city center. The 51-kilometer round trip ride to the Marken lighthouse will take you into the countryside just north of Amsterdam on a cycling path that runs atop a levy overlooking the brackish bays surrounding the city. Visit the official tourism site of Amsterdam, iamsterdam.com, for more information on citywide attractions and services.

were dying in record numbers. In 1971, 3,300 Dutch citizens lost their lives in vehicular crashes—including 400 children under the age of 14.

Protests against the marginalization of cyclists and pedestrians erupted across the country. Thousands of people gathered in the plazas where the cars once parked, carrying signs reading STOP KINDERMOORD, meaning "stop child murder." They painted renegade cycling lanes along roads. The government reacted by banning automobiles from many city centers and instituting nationwide car-free Sundays, an effort to save gas that also served as a reminder of what Dutch cities had looked and felt like before cars. Cycling lanes became permanent, and automobile lanes and parking spaces turned into separated cycling paths alongside the roads.

Today, when you throw a leg over a utilitarian Dutch bike and glide into the stream of cyclists rumbling along the wide brick cycle paths of Amsterdam, along the serene canals, past block upon block of romantic colonial revival architecture, you're riding in what's often ranked the top city for cycling in the world. Almost every major arterial roadway and bridge features separated cycling paths (400 total kilometers of them snake throughout the city). Many streets are entirely closed to auto traffic, and the speed limit on 900 kilometers of Amsterdam's roadways is a pedestrian 30 kilometers per hour. In the city's center, cycling makes up 57 percent of all traffic. All of this makes getting around by bike in one of the world's most culturally entertaining cities the best way to travel.

Basque Country

SPAIN

Technically, the Basque Country occupies a splash of northern Spain and a sliver of southern France. Yet, the Basque people, spread across the western mountain ranges of the Pyrenees and along the southern coast of the Bay of Biscay, do not strictly identify with either overarching nation.

The lineage of the fiercely independent Basque people traces back to the region's indigenous inhabitants, who over the millennia fought against rulers ranging from the Romans to Napoleon to the Spanish dictator Francisco Franco as late as the 1970s. After the death of Franco, the newly formed Spanish democracy granted the Basque Country its own autonomous government (it's one of 17 different autonomous governments in Spain), and for decades Basque nationalists dominated the regional politics.

However, today, with an influx of many non-Basque Spaniards to the region and the muddling of Basque and Spanish societies, the Basque Country has become more of a cultural identity than a political one. In 2011, the ETA, the violent Basque separatists that once terrorized the Spanish government,

Get There

▶▶ A number of touring companies offer fully supported Basque Country trips focusing on both cycling and cuisine. Two popular options include Velo Classic Tours (veloclassic.com) and the travel arm of the historic Basque bike company Orbea, which offers an off-road tour called the Fish and Wine Route (orbea.com). The Basque Country tourism season typically runs from June through October; however, beach towns such as San Sebastián can get crowded in August, when Europeans traditionally holiday. Visit tourism.euskadi.net for more information on lodging and dining options in the region.

laid down their arms. And in 2009, the Basque Country elected its first non-nationalist government. While Basque nationalism remains a contentious issue (don't bring it up at a dinner party), across the region you'll still hear children speaking the unique language of the Basque, Euskara, an idiom completely separate from those spoken in the entirety of Europe, with an as-yet-unidentified origin. At the bars and cafes in the bustling coastal cities of Bilbao and San Sebastián, you'll eat and drink the revered Basque cuisine, such as pintxos, the Basque version of tapas, and Txakolí, a deeply refreshing sparkling white wine. In the challenging but not intimidating mountains overlooking the sea, you'll find narrow, winding roads marked with signs reminding drivers to give 1.5 meters of space as they pass each of the thousands of people who participate in the Basque Country's most beloved sport, cycling.

It's unlikely that any other area in the world has produced as many top professional cyclists and Michelin-starred chefs as the Basque Country, and for this reason, there's perhaps no better place to go on a holiday with your bicycle. The five-time Tour de France winner Miguel Indurain claimed Basque heritage, and for nearly 2 decades the region boasted its very own Tour de France team, Euskaltel Euskadi, composed entirely of Basque racers and funded in large part by Basque cycling fanatics. Today, the Clásica San Sebastián, held the week after the finish of the Tour de France, in early August, is one of bike racing's most important 1-day events. The race attracts many of the tour's top finishers and throngs of passionate supporters, who line the slopes of the Alto de Jaizkibel, a gradual 8-kilometer ascent up a treeless mountain overlooking the deep-blue Bay of Biscay.

Summiting the Jaizkibel, replete with 19th-century stone garrisons at its crest, should have a place on any Basque Country itinerary. But so, too, must visiting the world-renowned pintxo bars found fronting the narrow streets of San Sebastián. Spaniards dine late, starting around 10:00 p.m., and spend the twilight hours winding up to the main course by hopping between pintxo bars, downing anchovies plucked from the sea and served on bite-size toast with myriad toppings or sharing a salad including fresh octopus, all while standing at a wooden bar sipping cocktails.

While many of the highest-rated pintxo bars and restaurants can be found in the Basque Country's major cities, for many cyclists the most memorable meals occur deep within the region's valleys and along its rural mountainsides. (Undoubtedly, the effort required to pedal to these places makes the food taste that much more wonderful.) Take, for example, the ancient trade route over the Basque Country's Urkiola mountain range that travels a mountain pass known as the Puerto de Urkiola. The pass holds a special place in Basque lore. For centuries it was used by merchants and missionaries who brought both cargo and Christianity from the coast toward Madrid. Today, the road perennially features in the tour of the Basque Country, and for patriotic Basque cycling fans, it is held in the same level of regard as the Tour de France's Alpe d'Huez, or the Giro's Stelvio.

The frequently mist-shrouded ascent, 5.7 kilometers long at an average gradient of nearly 10 percent, starts near the small town of Durango and climbs toward the highest peak in the Urkiola range, Anboto. At its precipice, this mountain features expansive hunks of sheer limestone, jutting hundreds of feet up from the forests and grassy plains toward the sky. After a grueling 400-meter-long, 14 percent pitch known as the Txakurzulo ramp, where the race up this mountain is most often decided, the climb culminates at a centuries-old sanctuary that now doubles as a hotel and restaurant. At the restaurant you can dine on local specialties such as blood sausage and imbibe bottles of Txakolí. Traditionally poured from high above, the sparkling white wine cascades like a waterfall toward the rim of your glass.

Well prior to the construction of the sanctuary (between the 8th and 9th centuries, it's estimated), the Basque people considered this mountain pass a sacred place, the dwelling of Mari, the main figure in Basque mythology. In an effort to spread Christianity along this trade route, many religious structures were built on Basque spiritual sites, caves, springs, and these pointed mountain peaks. But, as it's done for thousands of years, the Basque identity endured.

When the rain falls from high above this watershed mountain range, like the flowing Txakolí wine, it hits the peaked roof of the sanctuary atop the Urkiola pass and flows in two disparate directions: To one side, the water flows down the southern slope of the mountain, toward the Spanish capital of Madrid and into the Mediterranean Sea. To the other side, the water flows north toward the Bay of Biscay, and back into the Basque Country.

Berlin Six-Day Race

GERMANY

Ladies and gentlemen, step forth and behold, in all its splendor and brilliance, the most amazing, incredible, stupendous spectacle upon two wheels. Witness a show of men and machines, of lights and music and dancing, and beer! Yes, beer! Wonderful German beer! Please, come inside here, beneath the soaring steel girders of the Landsberger Allee velodrome. Take a seat among the 12,000 other screaming spectators. And ready your senses for a fantastic cycling circus.

Get There

▸▸ The Berlin Six-Day traditionally takes place in late January. Admission starts at 30 euros, and the event typically sells out each evening. Visit sechstagerennen-berlin.de for more information.

Turn your attention there, to the wooden racing track, the impossibly banked 250-meter oval, with the men on shiny bicycles that neither coast nor brake, performing their pre-race parade. Behold the iron men of bicycling, bedecked in their bright, silken jerseys, their wheels humming as they weave up and down the velodrome's wooden boards. Chests puffed out. Legs smooth and glistening.

Yes, ladies and gents (and you too, boys and girls, you're welcome on family day, Sunday afternoon), this is the Berlin Six-Day Race in all of its magnificence—the oldest race in cycling's oldest discipline. An event of history and prestige dating back to 1909, back to when Americans (yes, us Americans!) dominated these nearly week-long competitions of seemingly inhuman endurance and speed.

Perhaps you've heard of New York City's Madison Square Garden? Well, then, were you also aware that the garden was built specifically for 6-day track-racing contests? It's true. In the early 20th century, American 6-day racers commanded higher salaries and drew larger crowds than the era's biggest baseball stars. The Madison race, the two-man, tag-team bike race that defines these 6-day competitions, is named after that very stadium in New York City.

No American team has won the Berlin Six-Day in decades, but that hasn't stopped from trying. Look there, down on the track, and you'll see the stars-and-stripes-splattered jersey of Guy East, tall and slender and tan with a coiffed head of blond hair, tipping his trademark cowboy hat to the crowd, flashing a pearly white smile as the announcer bellows the racers' introductions.

"I view sport as entertainment, and myself as an entertainer," says East, and he strives to put on a good show for the fans. You see, the 6-day never fails to deliver blistering attacks, daring escapes, desperate chases, and down-to-the-wire finishes. (Consider the Berlin Six-Day the NBA All-Star Game of bike racing, combining elements of cutthroat competition and blatant showmanship.)

And now East, waving us down from the stands and onto the infield of the velodrome, shows us the tiny cabin (or "hut," as he calls it) where he can nap between the evening's events. Though the 6-day races long ago gave up the 24-hour format, the schedule still proves grueling, running from 6:00 p.m. well into the early morning hours. Racers like East compete in more than half a dozen Madison races each evening, topping speeds of 65 kilometers per hour during the all-out competitions.

The racers' cabins, East points out, take up only a fraction of the infield space. Over there, we see the white-linen tablecloths and long-stemmed wine glasses in the VIP area, where the backslapping and business deals take place. And there, up on the stage, beneath the swaying neon lights, are Cher, the Blues Brothers, and Queen, or at least the lovable German impersonators of these famous performers. Below the stage, you'll see dancers in denim and leather, intoxicated, without a care or concern for a bike race. Fog flows from the stage, hands rise and clap in unison, everyone sings along.

But the show must go on despite the blissful distraction, and so a man comes to rouse East and his competitors from their cabins. They take to the track for the main event, an hour-long Madison, in which the teams of two racers take turns slinging one another into the race, sprinting for points, and trying to lap the pack.

Ladies and gentleman, boys and girls, bike-racing aficionados, beer lovers, and rabid fans of European cover bands, this is the Berlin Six-Day in all of its glory, where a good time every night, for nearly a week, is always guaranteed.

Dalmatian Coast

CROATIA

Crystalline waters tinted in the hues of shimmering jewels, sapphire and topaz and emerald, ring the islands and fill the bays and coves of the Dalmatian Coast. If you ride a bike in this region, the southern half of Croatia, across from Italy along the eastern shore of the Adriatic Sea, you will ride up and over mountains of sheer limestone that jut from the ocean in imposing and alluring formations. You will pedal through an arid landscape eternally drenched in sun, through forests of cedar and pine and along rocky hillsides laden with golden shrubs. You will descend back toward the emerald sea on a series of switchbacks clinging to a precipitous cliffside and arrive in an ancient fishing village where clusters of whitewashed buildings are topped with red-tile roofs, and the crystalline waters will beckon to you: Come, climb in, swim.

The roughly half a dozen major islands of Dalmatia run in a line parallel to the coastline between the region's two major cities, Split and Dubrovnik. Thus, the most popular way to explore the Dalmatian Coast is by both boat and bicycle, riding each island from end to

Get There

▸▸ The capital of Croatia, Zagreb, is served by many European airlines and provides connections to both Split and Dubrovnik via Croatian Airlines. Ferries run between all the major islands along the Dalmatian Coast, and a single road typically runs along the spine of each island or borders the coastline, making route-planning relatively stress free. A number of tour operators, including Backroads (backroads.com), offer fully supported trips as well, using privately chartered boats. For a list of Dalmatian Coast accommodations ranging from chic hotels to lighthouses transformed into multiroom guesthouses, visit croatia.hr.

end—a distance of 50 to 80 kilometers, depending on the island—and then hopping on a ferry or privately chartered boat to reach the next island. From the medieval walled city of Dubrovnik to the glamorous resorts of Hvar Town to the beautiful but mostly untouristed island of Vis, seemingly untouched by time and technology, each ride and boat trip along the Dalmatian Coast promise new people, new food, and new cultures, all set against a similarly stunning backdrop.

DALMATIAN COAST

Tour of Flanders

BELGIUM

Imagine if kids played T-ball at Wrigley Field. If weekend warriors gathered for pickup basketball games at Madison Square Garden. Or if you could go throw around the ol' pigskin at Lambeau Field. If the hallowed grounds of a major American sport were basically your backyard ball fields, then you might understand what it's like to ride a bike in Flanders.

This northern portion of the country of Belgium—bordered by the North Sea to the north, the Netherlands to the east, France to the west, and the more rural Wallonia region to the south—is defined by its bike-path-lined canals, its sunken farmlands, and its historic centers of culture and commerce, Antwerp, Ghent, and Brugge. In these cities and the tightly clustered villages in between, you'll find purveyors of handmade Belgian chocolates (this nation claims to have invented the bonbon and even the chocolate bar) and Trappist monasteries where some of the world's best beer is brewed. Near the border with Wallonia, you'll also find that the terrain shifts. The flat coastal planes turn into forested hills known as *hellingen*. Centuries-old paths lined with big, rounded cobblestones are carved into the hills, jutting up from the surrounding pastures at grades as steep as 20 percent.

It's these cobbled climbs that draw Belgians, even as small children, to scramble toward the top on their bikes. It's here that they first learn to navigate the stones and develop the power needed to maintain traction on the slippery surface. It's here that they try to emulate the great Belgian cyclists such as Eddy Merckx and Tom Boonen on the very roads where these racers became legends. It's here, on these seemingly innocuous little roads, that every spring for the past

100-plus years men have inscribed their names in the history of the sport, and the nation.

Like many of the world's most important bike races, the Ronde van Vlaanderen, known to Americans as the Tour of Flanders, was conceived by a sports paper as a means of increasing circulation. First run in 1913, the design of the route has always called for a true champion of Flanders. Racers must muscle through the barreling winds that blow across the open fields, conquer the ancient road surfaces that mercilessly hammer skinny bike tires, and summit the hills that rise abruptly and cruelly from the pastoral landscape. The champion of the Tour of Flanders must prove representative of the hardy people of Flanders, immeasurably tough and determined, unfazed by inclement weather and unforgiving terrain.

The race, which has started in Brugge in recent years, is more than 260 kilometers long and features as many as 18 ascents of the cobbled hills of Flanders, which are brutally placed one after another in the latter half of the route. The part of Belgium where these centuries-old cobbled paths survive, hidden away in the hilly farmland, is a small area in a small country—primarily surrounding the banks of the River Scheldt and the town of Oudenaarde, where the Ronde currently finishes. In order to maximize the number of punishing trips up the *hellingen,* the course constantly twists and turns back on itself in a series of loops that leaves racers dizzy and the peloton strung out from the constant turns and undulating terrain. Nowhere else in the world do cobbled surfaces such as this exist, and nowhere else in the world is there a race like the Ronde van Vlaanderen.

Get There

▶▶ Oudenaarde, the current finishing town of the Tour of Flanders, is a 45-minute train ride from the Brussels international airport. In Oudenaarde you'll find the Centrum Ronde van Vlaanderen (crvv.be), a museum and visitors' center that tells the history of the race and encourages guests to get out and explore for themselves. The center offers maps of various signposted routes traversing the best-known climbs, as well as showers and a café and bar offering post-ride refreshments. Every year, on the day before the Tour of Flanders, recreational riders are welcomed to take on the route en masse during the Ronde van Vlaanderen Cyclo (sport.be/rondevanvlaanderen). The ride draws more than 16,000 participants, with spectators lining many of the hills to warm up their lungs (and livers) for the premier event the following day. Visit cycling-in-flanders.com for more information about the region, its cycling history, and the various breweries along the route.

The hills here are so revered—and feared—that adding one cobbled climb to the course and removing another can result in outrage and mass protest. Take the Koppenberg, just 600 meters long but kicking up to 22 percent in the middle, barely the width of a small car (race vehicles are now diverted around the climb during the Ronde since its return) and riddled with cobbles so ferocious it's not uncommon for riders to hoof their bikes to the top rather than ride. For this reason, the Koppenberg, frequently considered the opening salvo in the race's hostilities, has been intermittently excluded from and reintroduced into the Tour of Flanders since its inception in 1976. The longest exodus from the Koppenberg came after the 1987 race, when leader Jesper Skibby lost his momentum and veered toward the sharply arched center of the road just as the car of the race's chief commissioner attempted to pass. The car knocked Skibby to the ground and then drove over his bike, narrowly missing his long legs. The race finally returned to the Koppenberg in 2002, after the town of Oudenaarde restored the road and added 650 feet of new stones. Still, the climb remains on permanent probation, only heightening its legacy.

Conversely, when in 2011 a new promoter of the Ronde announced the removal of the Muur van Geraardsbergen—a circuitous climb that steepens and roughens as it rises toward a domed chapel at its crest and on which numerous Flanders champions have launched their race-winning attacks—the passionate Flemish fans howled in opposition. In mourning its removal, protesters, dressed in black and carrying coffins, staged a symbolic funeral procession up the infamous Muur, which means "wall" in the native Flemish dialect.

Every spring, thousands upon thousands of people gather to gaze in astonishment at cyclists as they suffer up these short but horrific climbs. The racers' arms are flexed over the handlebars, their legs bowed to the sides in agony, and their jaws agape, feeling like they're wrestling a jackhammer while pedaling up a wall of ice. On these hills, the racers give everything to try to win Flanders—or at the least, to save themselves from the ignominy of walking to the top. Then, the race finishes. The fans disperse, and these iconic roads return to nothing more than quiet backwoods paths infrequently traveled by vehicles. These humble, cobbled monuments wait for you to come here with your bike. Perhaps when no one is looking, if you build up a good head of steam (momentum is critical), you too can attempt to conquer the *hellingen* that exist only in this small area of this small cycling-mad country.

L'Eroica

ITALY

If you love bicycles, it's likely that you have a grandfather or a great-uncle or an aunt who also loved bicycles. It's possible that they bequeathed to you an old steel bicycle, a beautiful bicycle, long since exiled to the far corner of a garage or a cobwebbed attic. A bicycle once beloved, now abandoned in favor of carbon fiber, electronic shifting, and clipless pedals.

Find that bicycle. Polish it. Restore it to its original glory, and bring it to Italy. Specifically, come to the Chianti region of Tuscany to ride in L'Eroica, an event where the past returns to the present. At L'Eroica, a ride limited by lottery to only a few thousand participants (only a thousand or so foreigners), technology is eschewed and passion is celebrated. Participants are strictly prohibited from riding any bicycle manufactured after 1987—violators may be banned for life.

L'Eroica began in 1997 in the village of Gaiole. In an effort to preserve Italy's last remaining white gravel roads, its famous *strade bianche*, 92 locals, dressed in wool jerseys and leather helmets, pedaled 205 kilometers over the quilted hills of Tuscany, one of the world's most cherished cycling destinations. Since then, cyclists young and old (the old are given special preference) have flocked to L'Eroica to revel in and relive the stories that progress and technology left behind.

> ## Get There
>
> ▶▶ The ride starts and finishes in Gaiole in Chianti, Italy, in early October. The lottery for registration is open only during the month of February. Women and men over 60 do not need to enter the lottery and can register in March. Only official L'Eroica bicycles—built before 1987—are permitted in the ride. Visit en.eroica.it for more information.

At a fair preceding the ride, vendees dig through worn boxes full of old cycling components like chests of treasure, coddling 5-speed derailleurs like crown jewels. On display stand the hallowed steeds of the Italian cycling champions Gino Bartali and Francesco Moser, for whom L'Eroica ("the heroes") was named. Clustered together at the start, participants fondle the immaculate lugged-steel joints of handmade bicycle frames and adjust their head lamps for the predawn departure. Rest stops shun modern energy drinks, gels, and bars in favor of an assortment of cured hams and fresh berry tarts. Riders drink wine, both bubbly and red. At the finish, the white powder of the *strade bianchi* cakes the shins of proud, happy L'Eroica participants, who frequently finish the longest route, 200 kilometers, well after the sun has set.

After the ride, the finishers cluster together to share tales of their adventures, past and present (but mostly past), to swig Negroni beer from green bottles, and to watch all the other wonderfully historic cyclists watching them.

Majorca

SPAIN

Close your eyes now, and imagine a paradise for cyclists. Envision an island surrounded by jewel-colored waters, with terrain that varies from soaring stone mountains to rolling hills and agricultural plains. Listen to the soft hum of your tires on silk-smooth roads ascending cliffsides in enticing loops at ever-gentle gradients and back roads that are half a lane wide and pass through groves of ancient olive trees. Feel the warm sunshine against your skin, breath in the salty coastal breezes. Know, here and now, that such a place exists, and it is named Majorca.

Part of the Balearic Islands, in the Mediterranean Sea off the eastern coast of Spain, Majorca has long attracted vacationers seeking relaxation and beauty, and it is increasingly a coveted destination for road cyclists from around the world. Some of the top Tour de France teams, such as Sky, train here, yes. But from February through May, you'll also find packs of cyclists participating in all-inclusive camps, riding through the Tramuntana mountain range on the island's western coast and congregating in the plazas of the numerous tiny towns across Majorca.

> ### Get There
>
> ▸▸ Majorca is located roughly 200 kilometers from Barcelona on the eastern coast of Spain's mainland. Flights arrive in the capital city of Palma de Majorca, on the western side of the island. Many cyclists take a bus or taxi to the northeastern side of the island, near Port de Pollença, closest to Majorca's most popular rides. Dozens of companies offer cycling camps, organized rides, and bicycle rentals in Majorca. Visit seemallorca.com for more information.

> **"Sa Calobra rises from a deep cove of turquoise-tinted waters. As it ascends the side of a sheer canyon wall, clinging to the charcoal-colored rock face, the road loops back on itself in a series of almost comical curlicues."**

Sa Calobra, the most sought-out ascent on the island, rises from a deep cove of turquoise-tinted waters. As it ascends the side of a sheer canyon wall, clinging to the charcoal-colored rock face, the road loops back on itself in a series of almost comical curlicues, at one point crossing over itself in a figure eight via a stone bridge. With an average gradient of 7 percent over 10 kilometers, professionals testing their early-season form often ascend Sa Calobra in under 30 minutes, but that leaves little time to soak in the double splendor of engineering and scenery that's on display in the ride up this famous Majorcan mountainside.

At the far northeastern tip of the island, the Cap de Formentor peninsula juts into the Balearic Sea, providing a surreal cycling route on a slip of land bordered by the ocean to either side. The ride from the popular bicyclist base camp of Port de Pollenca, roughly 20 kilometers each way, twists through rugged coastal terrain before culminating with a switchback climb up to a historic lighthouse where you can look back toward the peninsula's rocky bluffs that lean toward the sea.

Majorca certainly isn't a hidden paradise, and perhaps the only knock against the island is that you'll share the terrain with scores of other riders who've come here for the same reason as you, to see what a heaven for cyclists might look like.

Mont Ventoux

The Giant of Provence, Mont Ventoux, stands alone, geographically disparate from the Alps and Pyrenees. On a clear day, the summit is visible from 100 kilometers in any direction. Above the lower-slung surrounding hills, the mountain's peak, completely bare of vegetation, appears all the mightier—a statue of a mountain, defying the local terrain.

The ride to the top of Ventoux—21.5 kilometers, rising 1,552 meters at an average gradient of 7.2 percent from the town of Bédoin—has brought the world's best bicyclists literally to their knees and in one dreadful case even resulted in death. Yet, it's not Ventoux's height, length, or steepness (with pitches above 12 percent) that have made the mountain peak—capped with a weather station that stands like a turret—a beacon for cyclists from around the world. In the Middle Ages, the mountain was scalped of its trees for lumber and reforested only around its steep base. Today, the final 7 kilometers of the road up the mountain rise through a vast field of windswept white limestone, a completely surreal moonlike landscape. The rocky peak not only makes Ventoux visually unique but also adds challenges infrequently encountered on France's other high mountains.

The mistral, a violent wind that blows from northern France into the Mediterranean Sea during the winter and spring, rips across the upper slopes of Ventoux. With no surrounding mountains or tall pines to buffet the wind, speeds as high as 320 kilometers per hour have been recorded by the weather station at the peak. The French *Mont Ventoux* translates to "windy mountain." Yet, the wind isn't the only unique concern for cyclists longing to summit Ventoux. In the summer, the white rocks reflect the sun, making Ventoux feel more like Mercury than the moon, a heat lamp atop a mountain peak. There's no shelter, no shade, no place to hide from the omnipresent sun for the final 10 kilometers on Ventoux, only a long, lonely road winding toward the summit.

Most cyclists know this mountain from the Tour de France. The race first ascended Ventoux in 1951. In the tour's 14 subsequent visits to the mountain, nine of which finished atop the peak, Ventoux hasn't failed to deliver dramatic moments. In 2013, Ventoux forced an exhausted Chris Froome to suck air from an oxygen tank after winning the vaunted stage atop Ventoux. The mountain starred in a dispute between Marco Pantani and Lance Armstrong, a spat derived from a stage win Armstrong gifted the egocentric Italian climber in 2000. Most notoriously, Ventoux claimed the life of British champion Tom Simpson in 1967, after he tumbled out of the saddle 2 kilometers from the summit. Dehydrated and ghostly white, Simpson reportedly told the spectators that came to his aid to "put me back on my bike." But the brandy Simpson supposedly swilled at the base of the mountain (racers once believed in the performance-boosting powers of sweet liquors), as well as the amphetamines later found in his jersey pocket, surely played just as much of a role in his demise as the punishing gradient and the windswept summit of Ventoux. In the year following his death, British supporters erected a memorial in the very spot where Simpson took his final gasping breaths.

Get There

▶▶ This being one of the world's most iconic cycling climbs, there's no shortage of cycling support available. You'll find bicycle outfitters situated at the base of the mountain at each town near Ventoux, and you can choose from rentals ranging from heavy hybrid bikes to an ultralightweight Pinarello Dogma with electronic shifting. Visit destination ventoux.com for a full list of outfitters and other local cycling routes.

Cyclists can ascend Ventoux on three sides, starting in the towns of Bédoin, Malaucène, and Sault. But it's the route from Bédoin that proves most challenging, and it's the one the Tour de France has used for all but the initial visit to the mountain, which set off from Malaucène. To clock an official climb, start from the roundabout in Bédoin, heading up D974, unmistakably signed as LA ROUTE DU MONT VENTOUX. The slope rises gently enough at first. Then, at kilometer 6, in the heart of the young but dense forest around the mountain's base, the gradient pitches.

Markers at each kilometer will tell you how far you've gone and, cruelly, the steepness at which the road ahead rises. Over the next 8 kilometers, the gradient averages well over 9 percent, and most riders will find themselves thumbing the shift lever, praying for one more easier gear.

The road bends to the left at kilometer 15 as it emerges from the forest onto the shallower but no less challenging slopes across Ventoux's bald peak. Here, there's a café, Chalet Reynard, with a cluster of road bikes around its deck. While the gradient eases slightly on Ventoux's upper portion, it's here that the wind and the sun will wreak havoc on any personal record attempts. Two kilometers from the summit, you'll pass Simpson's memorial, where riders have scrambled up the rocky embankment to leave trinkets, water bottles, and cycling caps honoring the fallen star, the Icarus of cycling. The final kilometer to the weather station kicks up again, a hard right-hand turn requires a few ferocious pedal strokes, and then you're done. A small store sells T-shirts and stickers, offering proof that a rider conquered Ventoux. But the unencumbered view is your true reward. On the clearest days, it's said, you can see the Mediterranean.

In the winter of 2013, the mistral winds blew so hard atop Ventoux that they knocked over the tall, granite Simpson memorial 2 kilometers from the summit—a sad but somewhat fitting event for a mountain that was once abused by humans who raped it of its ecology and that now exacts revenge on those who attempt to ride and race to its peak. Ventoux has been demonized (called the "evil beast") and mythologized since as early as the 1300s, when the noted Italian poet Francesco Petrarch wrote that Athos and Olympus seemed less incredible in light of the view from the summit of Ventoux. Every cyclist approaches Ventoux with her own perceptions, her own aspirations, her own demons, yet all share one thing: For those who arrive at the top, the mountain proves life affirming.

The Mortirolo, the Gavia, and the Stelvio

The Mortirolo, the Gavia, and the Stelvio: These three mountain passes rise above all others in Italy, both in altitude and in legend. The tiny, serpentine roads accessing these storied peaks wind through towering rock formations. They endlessly switchback up—up above the treeline, up above the clouds—into the craggy Italian Alps and the Dolomites, on the border of Switzerland. The Giro d'Italia, the Italians' version of the Tour de France, first made the cycling world aware of these climbs in the mid-1900s, but the roads—originally dirt paths—date back as far as the 18th century. From the village of Bormio, nestled deep amongst these Alpine peaks, a cyclist can ascend the Mortirolo, the Gavia, and the Stelvio. A masochist may ride all three passes in a single day.

Let us begin with the Passo di Mortirolo. Much has been said about this road, with its name derived from the Italian *morte*, meaning "death." A ribbon of asphalt that winds right up the valley wall, the Mortirolo's unrelenting ascent has been compared to a punch to the face. "Savage," says the great British sprinter Mark Cavendish of the Mortirolo. He calls it the hardest climb he's ever done. So does Lance Armstrong. The stats back up the hyperbole: 12.5 kilometers at an average gradient of 10.5 percent, with pitches as steep as 18 percent. The summit of the Mortirolo, at 1,852 meters high, is 900 meters lower in elevation than the Stelvio. Thus, dense forest mostly enshrouds the climb, and it lacks the sweeping treeless views of the grander Stelvio and Gavia passes nearby. But, as with all great climbs, it's the lore, the heroes who've risen—and fallen—on the slopes of the Mortirolo that cemented the mountain's place amongst the pantheon of must-rides.

The Mortirolo is best known, and even celebrated, for one of the most controversial cycling figures of the modern era, the diminutive Italian climber Marco Pantani. Four and a half kilometers from the summit, the sole retaining wall on the rustic mountain road bears a monument to Pantani, a man much beloved and much troubled during his enigmatic life. In the 1994 Giro d'Italia, in his second year as a professional, Pantani sailed clear of the five-time Tour de France champion Miguel Indurain on the Mortirolo, taking the crown of cycling's mountain king in the process. Following his win on the Mortirolo, Pantani endeared himself to Italian fans, the *tifosi*, with many more dramatic mountaintop victories, but he was also embroiled in unending drug scandals. In 2004, exiled from the sport and hopelessly depressed, Pantani passed away from a recreational drug overdose, a broken man.

Today, when the Giro visits the Mortirolo, thousands of fans line the impossibly steep slopes. They eagerly anticipate the first racer over the summit, the racer who is awarded the Cima Pantani, the Pantani summit prize. In honoring Pantani, and memorializing cycling's conflicted past, the Mortirolo reminds us that these mountains and the unyielding desire to ride up them ever faster can cause some cyclists to suffer long after they've reached the peak.

From the Mortirolo, a less harrowing descent leads to a valley and, after 14 kilometers of flat road, the village of Ponti di Legno. From here, the mighty Passo di Gavia rises. The road, narrow but almost perfectly paved, climbs for 17.3 kilometers and gains 1,363 meters in elevation at an average gradient of 7.9 percent. Since it was first introduced to the Giro d'Italia, in 1960, the severe and unpredictable weather at the high altitude where the Gavia tops out (2,621 meters) has produced some of professional cycling's most lasting images.

They called it the Day Big Men Cried, the day in 1988 when the Giro d'Italia raced toward the base of the Gavia pass through swirling mountain rain. American Andy Hampsten sat in third place overall that day and had planned to attack on the Gavia and make a bid for victory. Yet huddled together in the peloton, the racers shivered as they rode and sipped hot tea delivered by their team cars. Hampsten's competitors asked him, "You're not going to attack today, are you?" And he had

doubts. Could he endure the misery that surely waited on the upper reaches of the Gavia? For where there's rain in the valley, there's snow on the mountain.

But Hampsten had grown up in North Dakota ("riding 3 miles to school in the snow and 3 miles back") and logged thousands of training miles in the tempestuous Colorado Rockies. His American team, 7-11, had also come prepared. The morning

> **"The rain that once pelted him now came down in heavy, white snowflakes. He led the race, a minute ahead of his closest pursuer. He ascended beside walls of thick, gray rock and along the precipice of cliffs that seem to fall off into oblivion."**

prior to the stage, they'd scoured the town, buying up all the warm clothing they could find. As the racers began the climb up the Gavia on the fateful day, snaking through a series of switchbacks, the road narrowed to the width of a cycling path, and forest gave way to grassy slopes. In Hampsten's day, the top of the Gavia remained a dirt road, and when he felt the crunch of gravel beneath his tires and saw a sign warning of the upcoming 16 percent gradient, he accelerated.

Sure enough, the rain that once pelted him now came down in heavy, white snowflakes. He led the race, a minute ahead of his closest pursuer. He ascended beside walls of thick, gray rock and along the precipice of cliffs that seem to fall off into oblivion. Approaching the summit, he passed Lago Nero, a dark-watered glacial lake, and here a team manager held a bag of clothing, a jacket, scarf, and hat. His hands clad in bulbous neoprene gloves, his eyes shielded with Oakley sunglasses as big as ski goggles, Hampsten began the more gradual 25.6-kilometer return back to Bormio. Across the top of the summit, he raced past Lago Bianco, a translucent glacial lake. Like the opposing lakes, the yin and yang of the Gavia pass, Hampsten pedaled from dark toward light as he sped down the Gavia, flying through tunnels blasted into the side of the mountain and gaining minutes on his rivals. His arms shook uncontrollably and his gears caked over with ice, but at the finish in Bormio, he donned the race leader's pink jersey, a jersey he wouldn't relinquish.

In nicer weather, cyclists who make it to the top of the Gavia can stop at the Rifugio Bonetta for a coffee and a pastry. There, they can admire the many images from the Giro's visits to the mountain, the magnificent 3-meter walls of snow rising from the road to either side of the peloton and the deathly stares of the frigid racers. The race has come here seven times, always under apprehension from the race organizers, who've twice canceled trips up the Gavia, first in 1989 and again in 2013.

Where the Gavia ends in Bormio, the Passo dello Stelvio begins, rising northward to the highest mountain crossing in the Eastern Alps, at 2,758 meters. Called the greatest road in the world by the British auto show *Top Gear*, it's not just cyclists who know the Stelvio as an international marvel of mountain pass engineering. This being Italy, the road not only ascends the mountain pass but also does so beautifully. In 1819, at the behest of the Austrian Empire, which once controlled this sliver of the Alps, the Italian engineer Carlo Donegani designed and oversaw construction of the Stelvio. The road, 49 kilometers in total, took 5 years to complete (from 1820 to 1825), and in 1837 earned Donegani the title Nobleman of the Stelvio from Austrian Emperor Ferdinand I.

From Bormio, the road ascends the Stelvio for 21.9 kilometers, averaging a 7.1 percent grade and pitching to over 12 percent in the final kilometer before the summit. Intermittently located tunnels shield the road from rock falls but also bring long stretches of dimly lit riding (bring lights!). Waterfalls stream down cliffsides to a river flowing through the gorge below. Switchbacks, on which the road rises right up the mountain face, turn so tightly that they seem to overlap one another. Nearing the summit of the Stelvio pass, the Swiss border sits within a stone's throw to the north, and a lesser-known road, the Umbrail Pass (2 kilometers of which remain gravel) descends down into the neighboring country.

Get There

▶▶ Five different hotels in Bormio, all part of the Italy Bike Hotel group, offer special services for cyclists, including routes and maps, secure bike storage, laundry service, and in-room massages. Visit italybikehotels.com for more information.

Approaching the summit, the sense of utter remoteness disappears as a small village of taverns, cafés, and street-front shops emerges around a bend. The commerce taking place atop the Stelvio speaks to its popularity. Motorcyclists and car tourists lounge in the sun, enjoying a beer or two, while cyclists line their bikes up against café fences, wolfing down panini after 2 hours (or more) of continuous climbing.

Here, at the crest of the Stelvio, peering east into the green Adige River valley, the gloriousness of the Stelvio fully comes into view. The hairpin turns—48 of them over a 24.3-kilometer descent into Ponte di Stelvio—appear painted onto the mountainside, so great was the engineering artistry of Donegani. It's likely you won't be alone, standing at the waist-high, rock retaining wall overlooking the serpentine road below. Almost everyone looks out in wonder at the top, awed by the majesty of what they either just climbed or are preparing to roll down.

The Giro d'Italia first came to the Stelvio in 1953, taking on the climb from Ponti di Stelvio in the east and finishing on the opposing side of the pass in Bormio. That year, just as he'd done on Alpe d'Huez a year earlier, Fausto Coppi dropped his rivals to win the stage and secure the race's overall title. Coppi raced through walls of snow to win Italy's most important race on its most renowned pass, forever making the Stelvio the Giro d'Italia's most vaunted mountain climb. The race has visited the mountain 10 times since (with stages in 1984, 1988, and 2013 cancelled due to inclement weather). Today, the first racer over the top of the Stelvio, as Coppi was, is awarded the Cima Coppi, a revered prize befitting a revered mountain climb.

The Nürburgring

GERMANY

In the Eifel mountains of Germany lies a road referred to as the Green Hell by some of the best race-car drivers in the world. The road's hairpin turns and blind corners, shielded by dense forest, wind around the town of Nürburg and are perhaps the most famous 20.8 kilometers of tarmac in the world. For 1 full day each year, this hallowed racetrack belongs to bicyclists, who compete in a 24-hour relay bike race throughout the day and the night called the Rad am Ring. To join them, all you have to do is sign up.

Get There

▸▸ The Rad am Ring 24-hour race draws thousands of riders who compete as individuals or as part of a team but also offers shorter rides on the Nürburgring circuit for recreational riders. Visit radamring.de/en for more information.

Paris-Roubaix

FRANCE

The faces of Paris-Roubaix, pupils peering from mud and muck. Faces brought by a 255-kilometer-long race, 50 kilometers of which run over centuries-old stones that brutalize bikes and break bodies. This event makes little sense until viewed in the context of its history, its demented participants. It started with a velodrome in Roubaix, oval and shallow and built in 1895. Its builders hoped putting on a race would draw publicity away from Paris to the small town on the Belgian border, 280 kilometers away. "Child's play" for the hard men of the era, said the promoters, who scheduled the race as a warmup event for the then-vaunted 560-kilometer race from Bordeaux to Paris. No one set out to run the race over the most rugged cobbled roads there were in northern France; these roads just existed that way. The racers did all they could to avoid the stones, veering onto cinder cycle paths churned up into soup by the mass of riders. But then, as France rebuilt after World War II, the bombed-out cobbled roads were transformed with asphalt, and the racers and fans soon complained that Paris-Roubaix was losing its charm. So the promoters went looking for old roads, forgotten cobbled paths cutting across farms and fields, and then

Get There

▶▶ Roubaix is located 111 kilometers west of Brussels, Belgium. Every year, the Paris-Roubaix Challenge, is held on Saturday, the day before the professional race is run on Sunday. The ride, which attracts as many as 3,000 participants, offers routes of 170, 141, and 70 kilometers, including many of the most vaunted cobblestone sections, and finishes at the historic Roubaix Velodrome. Visit sport.be/parisroubaix for more information.

they rated them for their difficulty. How many wheels had these stones smashed? How many hands went numb from the jarring as their riders crossed these rounded rocks? The most famous and feared they rated five stars. Five stars for the Arenberg Forest, nearly 2.5 dead-straight kilometers through a tunnel of ominous trees and screaming spectators. It's said that this is not where the race is won but is often lost, and it's where the three-time Roubaix champion Johan Museeuw once fell and then nearly lost his leg to gangrene. Five stars for the Carrefour de l'Arbre, an atrocity of a road, just 20 kilometers from the finish, where the winners often make their move. And just one star for the final sector, a ceremonial 300 meters prior to the entrance to the velodrome and the historic 2.5 laps around the track that decide the winner. Every racer who's ridden and finished this race since its inception well over a hundred years ago has made this trip around the track. Every fan who has cheered from their sofa has wondered what it's like to sit in the stands at the velodrome, to have a pint at the clubhouse where the previous winners' names are scrawled above the bar, to hear the slapping of chains and flexing of spokes as men race over rocks maintained specifically for the running of this horrific event, and to see the anguished faces of the finishers. Every cyclist who has heard of this race has contemplated riding these cobblestones, pitted and slick and tossing the world's best cyclists from their bikes. To find out for yourself, there's only one place in the world to go: Roubaix.

Col du Sanetsch

SWITZERLAND

From the town of Sion in the canton of Valais, a sliver of pavement rises toward the high rock outcroppings of the Swiss Alps, seemingly going nowhere. The road, part of a mountain pass known as the Col du Sanetsch, does not continue down the opposing side of the mountain. There is no major destination at the top, such as a ski resort.

The climb up the Col du Sanetsch gains 1,770 meters over 26 kilometers, an ascent more imposing than many of Europe's most celebrated climbs, like the Passo dello Stelvio and Mont Ventoux. Yet, because no major races come here and because the road appears on a map to simply dead-end, few cycling tourists know this climb exists.

Will Davies, who documents the Swiss Alps' most spectacular mountains at the Web site cycling-challenge.com, calls the Sanetsch "a special climb" and says local riders view it as a secret treasure. Riding up this sliver of pavement from Sion up into the high Alps certainly feels as if someone let you in on a secret.

Get There

▶▶ Sion is served by connecting flights, with most major airports in Switzerland as well as by train. Visit siontourisme.ch for more information. Brevet Alpine Cycling Adventures (brevet.cc) features the Col du Sanetsch on its Gruyère cycling tour.

The climb of the Col du Sanetsch begins abruptly amidst the sun-drenched vineyards that flank the hillsides above Sion. As the ascent twists and turns up the mountainside at gradients approaching 20 percent, the entirety of the Rhône River valley comes into view. Far below, near the center of Sion, a medieval cathedral (which still welcomes parishioners) is perched atop a hill of stone rising from the banks of the Rhône River. Soon, the rows of grapes give way to a forest, the steepness of the climb fades, and a series of switchbacks ascends toward the tree line.

A long tunnel cuts through the cusp of the mountainside. Inside, water seeps from its ragged rock. Intermittent openings—large holes punched through the side of the tunnel, twice as high as a human atop a bike—act as windows, filtering in rays of sun and offering overlooks of the valley below. Today, automatic sensors light the way for cyclists and drivers making their way through the Sanetsch's dark and damp tunnel.

Where the tunnel ends, the smooth, narrow road continues through bright green alpine meadows dotted with colorful wildflowers. It crosses the cusp of the pass, with gray rock faces looming on either side and little fanfare, other than a small parking area, and then gradually descends toward a large, glistening lake, the Lac du Sanetsch, the reason for this road's existence. A hydroelectric dam formed this lake atop the Col du Sanetsch, and maintenance vehicles, in addition to a handful of tourists, are the primary users of the road up this imposing pass.

At the far end of the lake, there's an unlikely hotel and restaurant, the Auberge du Sanetsch. Here, you can toast your ascent with a beer or a glass of wine and dine on a spread of local cheeses and meats. And then, you can—in fact—descend down the backside of the pass, just not aboard your bike. There's a small cable car, the Sanetsch-Strausse, that carries passengers from the Lac du Sanetsch down into the village of Gsteig. A rack on the outside of the cable car allows you to dock your bike.

The cable car hangs over a towering rock face as it makes its way down into Gsteig, a rural village that is immensely Swiss, with classic chalet-style buildings and blossoming flowers adorning the fronts of homes. You can make a circuit of roughly 80 miles back to Sion by turning west, ascending two smaller mountain passes, the Col du Pillon and the Col de la Croix, and then following the Rhône River east, through the flat valley. Upon returning to Sion, you can look back toward the Alps, toward the Col du Sanetsch, and know that the secret of going up and over this giant pass is now yours as well.

Il Santuario della Madonna del Ghisallo

ITALY

To reach the steeple of the patron saint of cycling, the Madonna del Ghisallo, you must first have your sins absolved by climbing the route from the ice blue waters of Lake Como. Start at the tip of the peninsula that forks the lake into two halves like a split-tongued serpent. Peer out from the shore in Bellagio, the centuries-old vacation outpost of Italy's (and increasingly the world's) rich and famous. Geologically, the peaks rising from the shores of Lake Como are the foothills of the Italian Alps, yet they look—and on a bike, certainly feel—like imposing mountains.

From the shore, turn and ride through the narrow cobbled streets of Bellagio, past the Villa Serbelloni, once a mansion retreat for an aristocratic family from nearby Milan and now a five-star hotel, and look across to the western shore, the Gold Coast, where the morning sun awakens the water and surrounding mountainsides and billionaire celebrities enter bidding wars over lakeside villas. Find the Via Vallesina and begin the ascent toward the Santuario, pedaling away from the luxury and opulence and toward a higher, purer purpose.

The climb of the Ghisallo, 10.6 kilometers in total, starts steeply, snaking up the hillside at 7 percent, 8 percent, and then 10 percent. The road twists and turns through the woods, each bend providing breathtaking views (literally) of the lake, the mountains, and the Bellagio peninsula below. You'll ride past gated manses and rustic farm homes and into the hamlet of Guello, where the road flattens and then briefly descends into Civenna. Here, there's an overlook, a church, and a monument, but this is not the sanctuary of cyclists. It's fitting that, to reach the town of Magreglio, the home of the Madonna del Ghisallo, you must suffer just a little bit more.

In the final 2 kilometers to the summit the road kicks again, and three switchbacks, curving in divine perfection, deliver you to the peak of the misty mountain and the door of the sanctuary. Outside the chapel, the heads of Italian cycling, the campionissimos, Gino Bartali, Fausto Coppi, and Alfredo Binda, sit on stone pedestals, their busts cast in bronze. These three men dominated bicycle racing in Italy in the early and middle 20th century and long reigned over the Giro di Lombardia, the 1-day race honoring this region that takes place on the sacred roads circling Lake Como and is central to the legend of the Ghisallo.

The initial Giro di Lombardia occurred in 1905, but the Ghisallo climb, from Bellagio to the sanctuary at the summit, wasn't added until 1919. At the time it was an unthinkable monster of a mountain pass, and typically the deciding factor in the race. However, over time, the route up the Ghisallo was transformed from gravel to pristine asphalt, bicycle technology advanced, and the diets and training of racers improved (for example, it became unfashionable to chain-smoke cigarettes, as Bartali did). Over time, the Ghisallo became less decisive. Yet, every fall, even as the route of the Giro di Lombardia, the Race of the Falling Leaves, frequently changes, the Ghisallo remains the revered centerpiece of the event.

Long before this climb took on religious connotations, the race drew cyclists in droves. In 1944, a man named Don Ermelindo Viganò became the priest of the nearly 400-year-old Ghisallo chapel. Taking note of the stream of cyclists riding past the chapel, it occurred to Viganò to link the chapel with the race that annually passed by. He transformed the chapel into a shrine to Italian cycling champions, showcasing their bikes, jerseys, and trophies, and invited cyclists to take a break atop the Ghisallo to refill their bottles at the fountain and refresh their spirits. In

Get There

▸▸ Part of the beauty of the Santuario della Madonna del Ghisallo is its proximity to Milan, roughly 70 kilometers away. The bike ride from the busy city will take you through rolling farmland, along the shore of Lake Como, and up the Ghisallo. Whether you choose to base yourself in the fashion capital of Italy or one of the resort villages ringing Lake Como, a variety of guide services and bike shops are available to offer support. Visit lakecomo.it/en for more information.

1949, Viganò personally met with Pope Pius XII, who christened the Madonna del Ghisallo the patron saint of cycling. The pope blessed a golden torch that was relayed by bike from Rome to Lombardy. Both Bartali and Coppi carried the torch to the summit and then into the sanctuary, where it remains lit today.

The bronze bust of Viganò, who died in 1985, stands beside the likenesses of Binda, Bartali, and Coppi outside the chapel doors. Nearby, set against the backdrop of the mountains and the lake, a towering bronze statue depicts the conflicting glory and pain of the sport, one rider raising his arm in victory, another rider crumpled in defeat. The modern museum, constructed in 2006 on the grounds of the sanctuary, showcases the bicycles and tells the stories of the racers who climbed to victory on the Ghisallo, including the great Eddy Merckx, who won the Lombardia in 1971 and 1972. But it's the chapel, report those who've walked through the hallowed iron doors, where the truly chilling relics remain.

From the walls hang the pink and yellow wool jerseys of Italy's Giro d'Italia and Tour de France champions, respectively; the rainbow stripes of world champions; and wooden plaques honoring both the sport's great and its long-forgotten cycling champions. Most of the sport's most celebrated racers have made the journey up the Ghisallo too, to deliver these artifacts and take their place amongst their elite peers. Sadly, the artifacts of some champions made it to this chapel without them. On a ledge high above the chapel floor sits the bike of Italian Olympic champion Fabio Casartelli, its fork crimped backward from where it struck a stone wall during the 1995 Tour de France, flinging Casartelli down the mountain, ultimately to his death. With tragic incidents like this in mind, aspiring pros have been known to come here seeking the blessing of the Madonna—and to depart with a silver medallion bearing an engraved image of the Madonna encircled by a chainring (available in the gift shop)—and to pray that the patron saint of cycling will watch over them as they ride.

After climbing up the shrine to the Madonna, with its small prayer stools and rows of lit candles, regardless of religion, cyclists will find no holier place.

Sassetta to Suvereto

ITALY

First, the mosquitos called this place heaven. Before the Medici clan began draining the wetlands, the water pouring from the hills of Tuscany onto the coastal plains of the Mediterranean formed a brackish swamp. The bugs bred there—and then spread malaria. Anyone hoping to avoid the dreaded disease stayed far from this land, called the Maremma. And thus, it became a haven for outlaws.

Pirates trolled the shoreline and bandits roamed the inland valleys. While trekking through the Maremma in 1610, the master artist Caravaggio, the street-brawling bad boy of the Renaissance, caught malaria and died at the age of 38. The scattering of hearty residents who in ancient times managed to forge a living from the land (namely, the Etruscans) built their villages atop the wooded hills. The wetlands gradually dried, a project finally completed in the 1950s, and cattle were allowed to roam free over the coastal plains. The Maremma's Italian cowboys, the *butteri,* still round them up today and take them to the market.

The Maremma's torrid history has left it relatively free of crowds. Though tourism supports much of the local economy—the beaches are a favored summer retreat for native Italians—its wild west reputation endures. Foreigners who've heard of the Maremma likely know it from travel magazines as the undiscovered, forgotten, or secret Italy. With the malaria-carrying mosquitos and bandits gone and little auto traffic, cyclists now call the Maremma heaven on earth—in particular, one tiny road that winds down a hillside between two ancient villages, which just might be the best road for bicycling in the entire world.

Andy Hampsten first came to this road in the night. He was a professional

SASSETTA TO
SUVERETO

cyclist with the American Motorola team, and in 1988 he'd won the Giro d'Italia, Italy's 3-week-long national tour. Ever since that dramatic victory, he'd developed a deep appreciation for the country, its history, and, most of all, its roads. But on this evening, in 1990, he was tired and frustrated. He'd been driving all day from a race in the South of France to a friend's house in the hills of Maremma, where he would be staying and training for a few weeks. As he approached his friend's house, the twisting road through the forest forced him to creep along in his zippy European roadster. "It was just a dark tunnel in the headlights," Hampsten recalls.

The next morning, he awoke and got on his bike. He set off down the road, innocuously named Strada Provinciale dei Quattro Comuni, connecting the villages of Sassetta to Suvereto in the Livorno province of Tuscany, and soon, he couldn't stop smiling. At first, he reportedly thought, *Maybe I'm tired; maybe I'm just happy not to be in the car anymore.* Then, he realized, *This is the nicest road I've ever ridden.*

Over the 13 kilometers from Sassetta to Suvereto, the road gently bends 287 times—yes, 287 times, or a turn every 45 meters—and winds down a hillside at an ever-so-subtle 2 percent gradient. The sun streams onto the road through the tall canopies of cork trees. The bark is harvested from the trees to plug the bottles of red wine produced nearby, and their bare trunks, when dappled with Tuscan sun, turn a striking crimson. The road surface, 1.5 lanes wide, rides smoothly, like a placid lake in the iridescent morning. Every now and then, the trees give way to views of the surrounding countryside, exposing waves of rolling green hills that disappear into misty clouds.

Once a Roman settlement, the town's name, Suvereto, is derived from the Latin word for cork. The road up the hill was likely a path for donkey carts carrying cork peeled from the trees. The carts required a gradual slope, and so the path followed the contours of the hillside. Hundreds of years later, the path became a road and was paved.

In the early turns, you may consider grabbing your brakes. You'll brush the tips of your index fingers across the levers, and then you'll aim for the apex with just a soft squeeze. You'll realize that these turns aren't hairpins; they don't knock back your speed, force you to accelerate. They flow, from the exit of one turn—with a handful of elegant pedal strokes in between—to the entrance of the next. You'll shift your weight for the upcoming corner, lift your inside leg, dip your shoulder, and dive in. You've dreamed of riding roads like this, and now you are.

You may think about all you've done on a bicycle and wonder where this ride ranks. How the greatest pleasures we derive from cycling so often come from the challenges we conquer, the suffering we endure, how far or how fast we rode our bikes, what we discovered. Yet, in all the grandeur and adventure that cycling gives us, sometimes we forget the essence of the machine, the simple pleasures, the wonder of almost effortless bliss. Sometimes the perfect road isn't the one with the stunning view and the adrenaline-churning descent. It's not in the mountains or along the coast. It doesn't even have a memorable name. Sometimes the perfect road is the one that allows adults to play, to feel like kids again, to ride without any inhibitions.

After he retired from cycling, Hampsten bought a house near the road from Sassetta to Suvereto and started a bicycle touring company, Cinghiale, named after the local wild boars, which are the basis of much of the regional cuisine. Hampsten hosts tours in the Dolomites and on the white gravel roads of the Chianti region. But his favorite tours are here in the Maremma, soaring down the road from Sassetta to Suvereto. "Every time I ride it, I feel like I should've paid admission," Hampsten says. "I've ridden it probably a thousand times now, and it gets more fun each time."

> ## Get There
>
> ▶▶ The closest international airport is in Pisa, roughly 75 minutes north of Sassetta. Cinghiale offers 8-day tours of the area each year in mid-June. Visit cinghiale.com for more information.

When he's not riding with a touring group, Hampsten gets together with his local cycling buddies. They pedal from Hampsten's home in Castagneto, just north of Sassetta, down the Strada Provinciale dei Quattro Comuni to Suvereto, drifting through the corners and gesturing with their hands for emphasis in conversation. At a café in Suvereto, after about an hour of riding, they stop and have a coffee. They read the newspaper and relax until someone says, "Where to next?" They discuss the options, a few other splendid routes that pass along the coast or through a valley. But inevitably, they grin at one another. They get back on their bikes, and they ride back home on the tiny road that winds up a hillside between two ancient villages, and just might be the best road for bicycling in the entire world.

Saint Gotthard Pass

Four different routes rise above and below Saint Gotthard Pass, linking the German and Italian portions of the Swiss Alps. Two separate tunnels—one for trains, another for cars—burrow beneath the wide flanks of the mountain. A wide, modern road with its switchback turns impressively cantilevered away from the mountain provides a smooth drive for car-driving sightseers. And then there's the only route over the Gotthard Pass that's accessible to cyclists, an old road, a path forged through the mountains by the Romans in the 13th century and transformed into a cobblestoned carriage road in 1832.

The old road up the pass rises 12.7 kilometers through the Val Tremola, the shaking valley, and is almost entirely cobbled, from its base in the town of Ariola to its grassy summit at 2,106 meters in altitude. The surface of the Tremolastrasse, as it's called, isn't akin to the rough stones of Roubaix and Flanders. Here, the relatively small, tightly packed cobbles are arranged in a pattern of arches, leaving you with a feeling of admiration for the craftsmanship, and pity for the souls who laid them.

The cobbles may slow the ride up the Gotthard Pass, which ascends at an average gradient of 7.6 percent, allowing the rider more time to appreciate the road's 38

Get There

▸▸ The Tremolastrasse climb up the Gotthard Pass starts in the Italian-speaking Swiss town of Ariola, 123 kilometers south of Zurich and 161 kilometers north of Milan. In July, the 110-kilometer-long Granfondo San Gottardo starts in Ariola and takes on the cobbled ascent of the Gotthard Pass as well as the Col de la Furka and Col du Nufenen. Visit brevet.cc for more information.

hairpin turns that are stacked atop one another like a large ladder ascending the steep valley wall. The stonework of the Tremolastrasse—not only its surface but also the retaining walls securing it—allows the road to blend seamlessly with the surrounding alpine peaks and exposed rock faces, making it seem like a natural element of the mountainside. And because most motorists and travelers stick to one of the three other routes near the pass, you'll have this landscape mostly to yourself, just you, your bike, and the rattle of the rocks beneath your wheels.

SAINT GOTTHARD PASS

North America

MOAB, UTAH

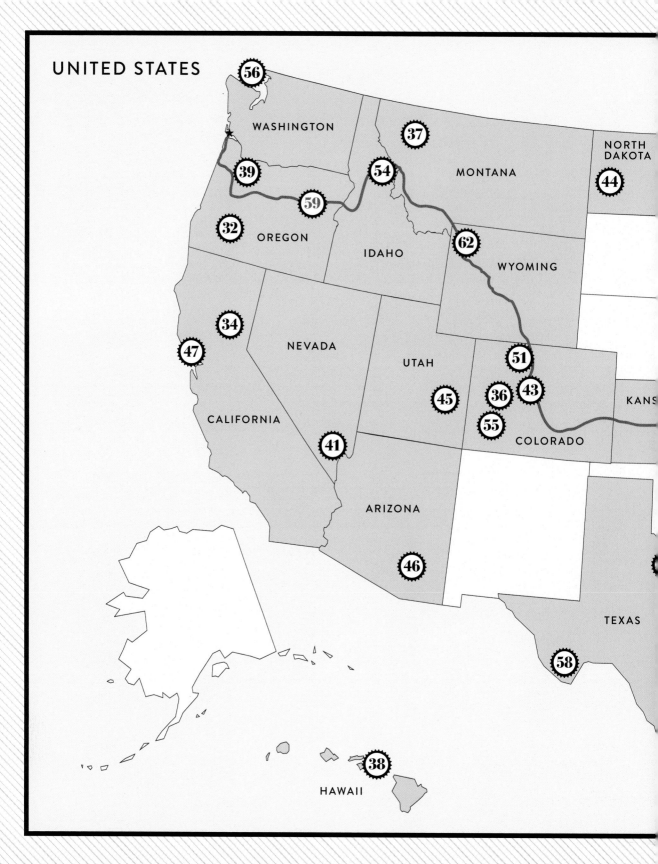

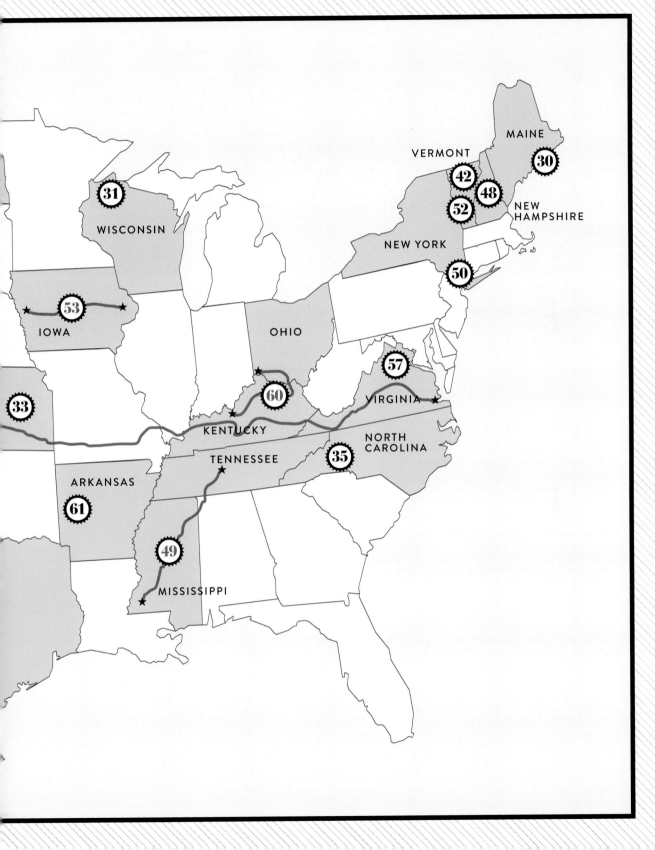

Cadillac Mountain

MAINE

Every morning from the fall through the spring, the first rays of sunlight to peek over the horizon fall on the slopes of Cadillac Mountain before anywhere else in the United States. Known as the definitive place to view the "nation's first sunrise," 1,528-foot-tall Cadillac Mountain is the tallest of 20 peaks clustered within the confines of Acadia National Park on the eastern coast of Maine. The mountain is also the tallest peak along the entire Atlantic coast of the United States.

Start your morning by making the 3.5-mile ride to the Cadillac Mountain's summit, a plateau of pink granite with views stretching out across the Atlantic Ocean. Then, continue along the 17-mile park road circling the base of the mountain and venture into the park's forested valleys and shoreline via a 45-mile network of car-free carriage roads that were built by John D. Rockefeller Jr. in the early 1900s.

Get There

▸▸ The tourist hub of Bar Harbor, Maine, located on Mount Desert Island (yes, that is the name of the island), is a popular jumping-off and landing point for adventures in Acadia National Park. Visit nps.gov/acad for more information about Cadillac Mountain and riding in the park.

Chequamegon Fat Tire Festival

In 1973, the owner of the Telemark cross-country ski lodge in tiny Cable, Wisconsin, decided to put on a marathon ski race in the style of the storied Birkebeiner Nordic event. The course wove through the dense woods of the Chequamegon (SHUH-WAH-MUH-GUHN) National Forest and across the rugged landscape of northern Wisconsin. Skiers who attended the race found that the fingers of ice that carved the earth here millions of years ago, leaving behind miles of lumpy hills and glacial depressions, made for perfect cross-country terrain.

The race, called the American Birkebeiner, grew quickly, resulting in the creation of a network of cross-country skiing trails stretching from Cable to the town of Hayward, 30 miles to the south. Within a decade, the American Birkebeiner became the biggest cross-country skiing race in the United States, and local organizers began to wonder, *What if we did the same thing, but on bikes?*

Thus, in the fall of 1983, just as the nascent sport of mountain biking began sweeping the country, 27 people signed up to race 40 miles from the store-lined streets of downtown Hayward to the Telemark Resort in Cable on a course composed of the Birkebeiner trail along with the primitive roads through the Chequamegon-Nicolet National Forest. The next year, 90 people came, and the year after that, 300. Racers found the event challenging but not too challenging. The Birkebeiner trail's 50-foot wide swath of manicured grass cutting through tall stands of pine, allowed large groups of racers to flow smoothly without log-jamming, appealing to both newbie mountain bikers and experts alike. The communal vibe of the event, which included various family-friendly activities like a mountain bike orienteering competition, kept people coming back and telling their friends.

Before long, the legend of the Chequamegon Fat Tire Festival had spread across the United States. There was, for example, that time in 1986 when mountain biking pioneer Joe Breeze called the Chequamegon 40 the "best bicycle event, period." Then there was the time in 1990 when Greg LeMond, fresh off winning a third Tour de France title, showed up out of the blue, did his very first mountain bike race in the pouring rain, and won. And that perhaps most legendary time in 1991 when Beth Bertleson won the Klunker Toss by flinging an old beater bike 87 feet and 6 inches, besting the previous records for both men and women by more than 28 feet. Eventually, the Chequamegon festival grew so popular that organizers were forced to cap participation, today limited to 3,100 riders, who are selected by lottery.

For more than 30 years now, thousands of folks have come to this remote part of Wisconsin, where 85 percent of the land is covered in forest and there are fewer than 10 people per square mile, to race mountain bikes on ski and snowmobile trails and double-track roads carving through a glacial wilderness and then compete in events such as the Klunker Toss, Lumberjack and Jill Log Pull, and Bicycle Limbo. It's about as much fun as you can have on a bicycle, if you're lucky enough to get in.

Get There

▸▸ Cable is located 164 miles from Minneapolis and 299 miles from Madison, Wisconsin. You'll find plentiful options for accommodations in the Cable-Hayward area, as the local economy is primarily driven by recreational tourism, in addition to the timber industry (Hayward is also the sight of the Lumberjack World Championships). The growth of the Chequamegon Fat Tire Festival resulted in the creation of the Chequamegon Area Mountain Bike Association, which maintains a network of over 300 miles of trails and is a bronze-level-rated International Mountain Bicycling Association Ride Center. Visit the Chequamegon Fat Tire Festival's Web site at cheqfattire.com for more information about area lodging and the expansive trail system.

Crater Lake

OREGON

Cyclists can thank a volcanic eruption (40 times more powerful than Mount St. Helens's 1980 eruption) 7,700 years ago for one of the most stunning road rides in the United States. The undulating 33-mile Rim Drive loop within Crater Lake National Park provides alternating views of the lake's mirror-like blue waters and snowcapped Cascade peaks. The road bends through stands of Douglas fir and features 33 different pull-offs where cyclists can stop to enjoy the scenery and—at an elevation topping out at 7,100 feet—take a moment to catch their breath.

Get There

▸▸ Entrance to Crater Lake National Park is $10 per vehicle or $5 per person and $10 per family if bicycling into the park. During two Saturdays in September, the east side of Rim Drive is closed to car traffic. Additionally, the road is closed to automobile traffic during the winter but open to cyclists when the road is clear. Visit nps.gov/crla for more information.

Dirty Kanza 200

KANSAS

First, there's the distance: Take your traditional feat of cycling endurance, the century ride, and double down. Not 100 but 200 miles. With this change, the race moves from the realm of "I can do that" to "Can I do that?" Second, the hills and the wind and the sun: otherwise known as "the elements." Unrelenting. It's gotten as hot as 103°F out there. It's blown as hard as 25 miles per hour and more, leading to post-race reports that describe "soul-crushing" and "relentless walls of wind." It's always up and down on the ever-rolling mounds of the deceptive prairie land—those hills, they look easy until you're upon them—sapping your momentum, your strength. Third, there's the gravel, the gray, chalky shards of tire-shredding gravel that are the limestone and shale remnants of a shallow sea that covered this land, called the Flint Hills, hundreds of millions of years ago. The gravel is the reason the native grasses still grow tall and splendid here (because nothing else grows amidst all of this rock). In this corner of Kansas, surrounding the town of Emporia, you'll find the last of the once-great Great Plains, before they were plowed and tilled and turned into a dust bowl. You'll see the plains as they were when the buffalo still roamed. Pedaling across this landscape—once inhabited by the warring, buffalo-hunting Kanza tribe—you'll feel far, far away from the modern world, with its conveniences and its

Get There

▶▶ Emporia is located 89 miles from Wichita, Kansas, and 107 miles from Kansas City. Registration for the Dirty Kanza 200, which is held in May, opens online in January and sells out quickly. Visit dirtykanza200.com for more information.

distractions. The sound of the crunch comes up from the gravel, the crushed rocks beneath rubber tires, the meditative, monotonous, mesmerizing sound that you only hear when you're rolling forward.

In 2006, just 34 brave cyclists signed up for the inaugural Dirty Kanza 200. Today, the event sells out months in advance, and 1,500 riders pack the streets of downtown Emporia for the sunrise rollout. They come from various states and countries to ride the gravel roads so unlike gravel roads anywhere else in the world. They come increasingly on drop-bar gravel grinders, built for just this purpose with wide tires and disc brakes and bags to carry food and tools (the support stops come only every 50 miles). They come to test themselves against the inhuman distance and the unrelenting elements, the hills and the wind and the sun. They come to hear the crunch of the gray rocks of the Flint Hills of Kansas.

"In this corner of Kansas, surrounding the town of Emporia, you'll find the last of the once-great Great Plains, before they were plowed and tilled and turned into a dust bowl."

Downieville Classic

CALIFORNIA

They came here more than a century and a half ago, the original '49ers, in search of gold amidst the alpine peaks of California's Lost Sierras. Led by a Scottish adventurer and prospector, Major William Downie, they built a town at the confluence of the crystal-clear Yuba and Downie Rivers that flowed down through the valleys. By the 1850s, the town, dubbed Downieville, boasted 5,000 inhabitants and a number of thriving businesses. But as these things go, the gold soon ran out, the mines closed, and Downieville declined, only surviving because of its designation as the seat of the Sierra County government.

Then, decades later, modern-day explorers began descending on Downieville. They came for a treasure of their own, the paths into these wild mountains first forged by the miners a century earlier and maintained over time by the US Forest Service. The trails proved perfect for mountain biking, and soon word spread of this tiny town high in the Sierra Nevada. In 1995, local mountain biker Greg Williams created a race to showcase and celebrate the trails encircling the Downieville area.

The 28-mile point-to-point race, the Downieville Classic, starts in Sierra City, 12.5 miles east of Downieville, and climbs high into the Sierra Buttes on a rugged forest road, gaining more than 3,000 feet in 8 miles, then drops back into the center of Downieville on a series of singletrack trails, flowing through the forest, traversing technical rock gardens, and cutting across the steep faces of the mountain sides. As the classic grew, Williams added a 16-mile downhill event, regarded as one of the world's longest and most physically and technically demanding downhill runs. These Downieville courses have gained a reputation for anointing champions who epitomize the essence of mountain biking, riders who possess both astounding stamina and silky-smooth bike-handling skills. Every year, racers arrive from all over the world to test themselves on the trails of Downieville, which has grown into one of the country's biggest and most unique off-road festivals. Downieville's All-Mountain award—in which racers must complete the cross-country and downhill races on the same bike, with the top-cumulative-placing person winning—is one of the sport's most coveted trophies. But there's more to the Downieville Classic than just racing. The Classic's family-friendly festival includes bike demos and an expo, live music and beer, and a bike ramp on the banks of the Yuba River for riders to launch themselves sky-high, performing acrobatics before splashing into the icy-cold water.

The success of the Downieville Classic has proved instrumental in reviving this once failing mining town by bringing it national attention as a mountain biking hub. Today, a number of restaurants, bars, and lodges line the streets of Downieville, aiming to cater to the mountain bikers who arrive for the classic and also come year-round to explore the seemingly endless riding options. The nonprofit Sierra Buttes Trail Stewardship maintains and expands the regional off-road trail system. Funded in part by the Downieville Classic and other local events, the Stewardship employs a full-time crew of trail workers and operates a local outfitter, Yuba Expeditions, which provides shuttle services, bike rentals and repair, and trail info.

Here in Downieville, long after the miners arrived looking to plunder the mountains for their resources, a community of trail stewards evolved and created a community focused on protecting and expanding a new and more sustainable resource, the vast trail system, for everyone to enjoy for centuries to come.

Get There

▸▸ Downieville is located 103 miles from Sacramento and 89 miles from Reno, Nevada. The Downieville Classic cross-country race is limited to 800 entrants, and the All-Mountain competition, which includes the downhill race, is limited to 200 entrants and sells out quickly. Visit downievilleclassic.com for more information.

DuPont State Forest

NORTH CAROLINA

In 1996, thanks to a generous bargain sale from the DuPont Company, the State of North Carolina acquired 7,600 acres of dense forest in the heart of Appalachia's Blue Ridge Mountains. Even by Blue Ridge standards, the land proved breathtaking. The crisp waters of the Little River tumbled through thick stands of old growth oak and willowy white pine. Fern-laced granite domes rose from sandy creek beds, and slabs of gray rock jutted from the hillsides. Each autumn, turning leaves swelled across the vast upland plateau.

Get There

▸▸ DuPont State Forest is 115 miles west of Charlotte, North Carolina, and 15 miles southeast of Brevard. Visit mtbikewnc.com for the latest trail conditions, route suggestions, and directions to access points.

But the heart of the forest and its three pummeling waterfalls, prominently featured in films such as *The Last of the Mohicans* and *The Hunger Games*, remained under private ownership. In 1999, when the 2,200-acre tract of land containing the falls was sold to a real estate developer in a private auction, a contentious battle ensued. The state, backed by environmental groups with broad public support, fought for public access and conservation of the falls. But the developer pushed forward with plans for a slew of residences and began building a large road system.

In 2000, with both sides deadlocked, the governor of North Carolina boldly invoked the state's power of eminent domain, seizing the property and all three waterfalls and opening the entirety of the forest to the public for the first time.

Amongst mountain bikers, DuPont State Forest's unique ecology quickly gained a reputation as one of the East Coast's premiere destinations—best known for its one-of-a-kind slickrock trails, which traverse the forest's tall, granite domes.

The nearly mile-long Big Rock Trail climbs 500 feet up a wall of sheer stone (and yes, there are big rocks). Riders must muscle up and over giant boulders before reaching the payoff, a bald summit with a near 360-degree view of the forest below. Even when wet, the tacky, scouring pad–like granite provides abundant traction while the sandy soil on adjoining trails drains quickly, making DuPont a favorite destination for locals riders after rainstorms, a frequent occurrence in western North Carolina.

The Cedar Rock Trail descends back down the steep rock face, sending you slaloming past cairn markers and spongelike lichen before dumping you out onto a wide path adjacent to the Little River, and within in earshot of crashing water.

At Bridal Veil Falls, the forest's Little River cascades from a 4-foot-high over-hang, then splays out across a wide rock face, forming the immense veil of the bride. Here, movie buffs can mimic a scene from *The Last of the Mohicans* by crouching beneath the waterfall's ledge and shuffling through a tunnel composed of stone and water—the roar of the river, tumbling from the overhang in thick white sheets, contrasting with the forest's quiet serenity.

DuPont's 80-plus-mile network of singletrack, laid out in a web of nearly 100 different trail segments, is best explored with the aid of a guide, good local intel, or a great map. You can source all three of these at the Hub and Pisgah Tavern, located just north of nearby Brevard, a quaint town eager to cater to adventurous travelers.

At the Hub, the bike shop and the bar are one and the same. At the service coun-ter, locals and visitors congregate to share fresh pints of beer from a rotating assort-ment of local breweries and stories of knobby-tired exploits in DuPont.

401 Trail

COLORADO

There's some debate, sure, but Crested Butte, Colorado, makes a firm case for being the place where the mountain bike was invented. The story goes that the dirt streets of the funky ski town were so potholed that locals gave up trying to drive around town and instead unearthed old balloon-tired cruiser bikes to navigate the rough roads. A culture arose around the bikes, and soon gangs of riders began venturing up into the Rocky Mountains surrounding Crested Butte—most famously, over the 12,705-foot summit of Pearl Pass and into the neighboring mountain town of Aspen. Eventually, the Crested Butte crowd linked up with a fellow crew of mountain bike pioneers from Marin County, California, and added gears and knobby-treaded tires to their steeds. As the new sport of mountain biking took off, Crested Butte became a mecca. In 1983, local riders formed the Crested Butte Mountain Bike Association with the mission of expanding and maintaining the extensive trail network that exists up in the mountains encircling the town. To breathe in the thin mountain air here is to breathe in the very soul of mountain biking. And if you come, you must

> ## Get There
>
> ▶▶ Crested Butte is a roughly 4½-hour drive southwest of Denver. Crested Butte Mountain Bike Week, deemed the longest-running mountain bike festival in the world, takes place each summer and includes events such as a chainless downhill race, a 40-mile cross-country ride, and a 24-hour race that circles the various bridges of downtown Crested Butte. For more information about the town's trails and the latest trail conditions, visit the Web site of the Crested Butte Mountain Bike Association, cbmba.org.

ride the 401 Trail, undoubtedly Crested Butte's most iconic stretch of singletrack. Regularly acknowledged as one of the best trails in the country, the 401 follows a dirt road out of town, along the banks of the East River through a deep valley. Between the towering, treeless peaks of Mount Baldy and Mount Belleview, you'll begin the ascent of Schofield Pass, eventually veering right onto a steep singletrack trail that switchbacks up the side of the mountain before emerging above the tree line. From here, the 401 flows along the midsection of the mountainside, a ribbon of dirt cutting across grassy slopes and through thick fields of flowers and overlooking the lush valley below. You'll ride through stands of aspen and pine, across cold mountain streams, and down seemingly endless, flowing descents. You'll quickly understand why, with terrain like this, the inhabitants of Crested Butte were inspired to create a bike on which to go explore the mountains.

Going-to-the-Sun Road

MONTANA

There's a legend about this road and how it got its name. According to a press release issued on the day of the road's unveiling in 1933, the deity Sour Spirit descended from the sun to pass on the knowledge of the hunt to the young braves of the Blackfoot tribe. To provide further inspiration, while going back to the sun, Sour Spirit emblazoned his image atop a mountain, which became known as Going-to-the-Sun Mountain. Today, that mountain sits within the confines of Montana's Glacier National Park, along the Going-to-the-Sun Road, a route constructed specifically to showcase this mythologized land. Going-to-the-Sun Road spans 50 miles end-to-end through the heart of the national park, ascending 3,000 feet to the summit of Logan Pass, through green valleys filled with iridescent lakes and beneath jagged stone peaks jutting skyward like shark teeth. Within this wilderness, grizzly bears frolic in the snow while mountain goats and bighorn sheep forage atop Logan Pass. Where the narrow road hugs the side of the mountain, the speed limit is a cyclist-friendly 25 miles per hour, and frequently portions of the road are completely closed to traffic while remaining open to cyclists and hikers. Today, Going-to-the-Sun Road is just as legendary as it was in 1933.

> ## Get There
>
> ▶▶ Going-to-the-Sun Road runs between US Highway 89 and the town of West Glacier on US Highway 2, 189 miles north of Missoula, Montana. The unpredictable weather and precipitation of the Rocky Mountains necessitate regular plowing, and portions of the road are frequently closed for snow removal. Visit nps.gov/glac for the latest road conditions, as well as information on accommodations within Glacier National Park.

Haleakala Crater

HAWAII

On the island of Maui, where a volcanic crater rises 10,023 feet from the Pacific Ocean, you can pedal from the sea to the sky. The aptly named Crater Road traces the slope of this volcanic mountain, 38 miles from the sea to the summit at a steady 5 percent gradient. It takes many cyclists 5 hours or more to pedal to the top, climbing through half a dozen eco-zones, overlooking the pillowy tops of white cumulous clouds, and finally arriving at the barren peak of volcanic rock. The mountain is a national park, and a small visitors' center at the summit describes the geologic history of Haleakala, the magma that bubbled up from Earth's core thousands of years ago, forming this massive peak and leaving a sculpted landscape of rock formations shaded in rich reds, deep blacks, and toasted browns. The cyclists who make it here earn the ultimate reward: a bike ride back down smooth asphalt and gentle hairpin turns that takes just 75 minutes.

Get There

▸▸ The climb up Haleakala begins on the north coast of Maui, off the Hana Highway, near the town of Paia. Where Hanamu Road merges with State Highway 377, Haleakala Highway, a national park sign reads: 22 MILES TO THE CRATER AT THE SUMMIT, NO FOOD, NO WATER. Bring ample fuel for the ride to the top of Haleakala and come prepared for inclement weather, with warm clothes for the cold air at the top of the climb and the chilly ride back down. In June, cyclists participate in a mass gallop to the top of Haleakala during the Cycle to the Sun race. Visit cycletothesun.com for more information.

Historic Columbia River Highway

OREGON

More than a century ago, two Oregon men shared a vision to build a grand thoroughfare, a road that would run alongside the tall cliff faces overlooking the Columbia River Gorge, cutting across mountains and forests and past cascading waterfalls. Samuel Hill, a prominent lawyer and advocate of scenic roads, and Samuel C. Lancaster, an engineer and landscape architect, believed that this road would be the King of Roads, combining a key transportation corridor with the beauty of the Columbia River Gorge. "Men from all climes will wonder at its wild grandeur when once it is made accessible by this great highway," Lancaster wrote in endorsing the plan. The two men were part of a movement across the United States to bring the natural wonders of the country to a newly mobile public. The aesthetically engineered roads in Glacier and Yellowstone National Parks were built during the same era.

Hill rallied investors to support the project, and Lancaster designed a road that carefully considered the natural landscape, blending the stone retaining walls and bridges with pedestrian facilities and other scenic features along the route. In 1922, after nearly 10 years of design and construction, the road connecting Troutdale, just east of Portland, with the town of The Dalles, nearly 75 miles farther east, was finally completed. Regarded as the first scenic highway in the United States, the route drew hordes of sightseers to the Columbia River Gorge and also became a key lifeline for commercial and agricultural interests in central Oregon, delivering goods and produce to the coast.

But by the 1930s, the road began to suffer from its own popularity. Heavy truck traffic caused the asphalt to quickly deteriorate, and motorists concerned with getting

HISTORIC COLUMBIA
RIVER HIGHWAY

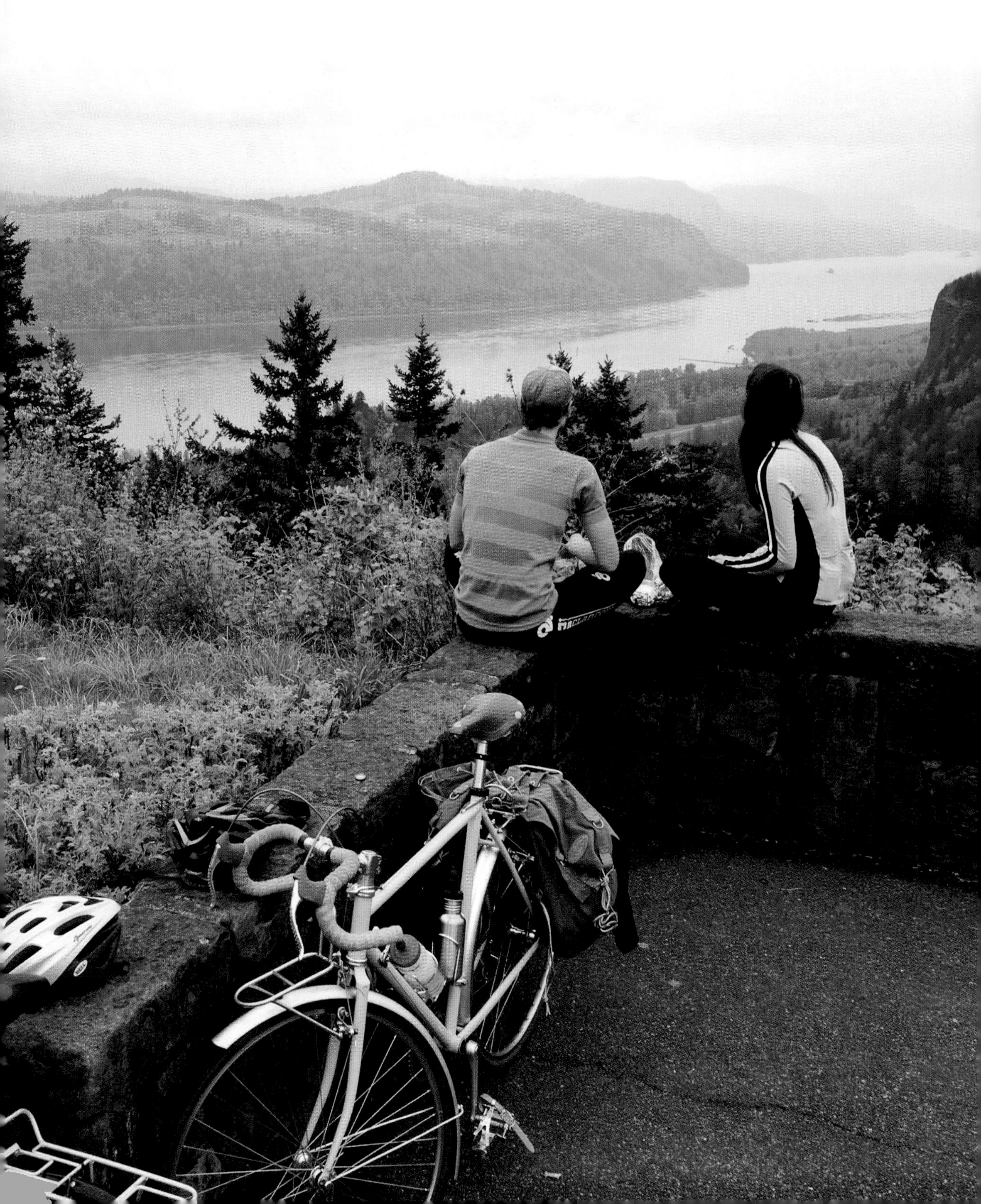

from point A to B as fast as possible conflicted with slow-moving tourists taking in the splendor of the Columbia River Gorge. Soon, new road projects aimed to bypass the Historic Columbia River Highway. Parts of the road were paved over during the creation of Interstate 84. The section of road featuring the Twin Tunnels, once considered an architectural marvel, was shuttered and the tunnels sealed off with piles of rock.

The King of Roads had fallen, but from the rubble the king of bike trails would rise. In the 1980s, the National Park Service led a restoration of the Historic Columbia River Highway as an extended bike route and tourist attraction. Today, two of the road's most scenic and historically significant sections serve as bike trails, completely closed to automobiles. The 3.5-mile section of trail between the Tooth Rock and Cascade Locks trailheads includes the Tooth Rock Viaduct. Part bridge, part cliffside road, the viaduct clings to the steep slopes of Wauna Point, overlooking the wide Columbia River. Farther east, the 5-mile Twin Tunnels trail segment begins just outside the town of Hood River. In 2011, when the Hood River Classic stage race used the trail as part of a time trial, competitors called the unique course one of the most dramatic they'd ever encountered. The former highway features gently graded climbs that ascend the steep hills in looping switchbacks, tunnels blasted from the rock and sealed in wood, and stone guardrails bordering a precipitous drop into the deep Columbia River Gorge.

Efforts to extend and create new trail segments are ongoing, with the ultimate goal of fully restoring the Historic Columbia River Highway to its original glory—but this time as a bike route, perhaps the best way to appreciate the natural environment.

Get There

▶▶ Hood River, located about 60 miles east of Portland, provides an ideal location for exploring the Historic Columbia River Highway and the surrounding area. In addition to the Tooth Rock and Twin Tunnels trail segments, you'll find miles of quiet country roads and an expansive network of mountain biking trails. Other popular outdoor activities include river-rafting and kitesurfing, as winds blowing through the gorge sometimes reach speeds of 35 miles per hour. Head to the Dirty Fingers bike shop and bar for additional local intel and $3 pints of local IPAs during happy hour. For more information about the Historic Columbia River Highway State Trail, visit oregonstateparks.org.

The Hotter'N Hell Hundred

TEXAS

This is what the sunrise looks like at the gates of hell. Flickering rays of light break over a long, flat horizon. A crescent formation of Air Force planes flies over a luminescent sky. Men and women adorned in pioneer dress huddle around a frontier-era cannon. Then, at 7:00 a.m. sharp, one of these frontier-era reenactors, Tree Wood, a giant man in a weathered leather hat who has presided over the ceremonial start of the Hotter'N Hell Hundred century ride for more than 30 years, lights the cannon's fuse.

At the sound of the ear-rattling boom, 13,000 cyclists who've congregated amongst the low-slung skyscrapers of downtown Wichita Falls, Texas—spilling into side streets and crowding onto sidewalks—surge forward, past an inflatable banner reading HELL'S GATE over the rusty brown Wichita River, and out onto the 100-mile route of the largest single-day century ride in the United States.

The landscape surrounding this town of 100,000 residents on the lower outskirts of the Texas Panhandle is composed of endless brown fields dotted with methodically pumping oil derricks, scrubby mesquite trees, and the occasional, blessed grove of Texas live oaks. When cyclists daydream of places to ride a bicycle, they tend not to imagine a landscape such as this, especially in late August, when

Get There

▸▸ The Hotter'N Hell Hundred traditionally takes place on the last weekend of August. Registration opens January 1. Wichita Falls is located 2 hours northwest of the Dallas–Fort Worth airport. Lodging fills up months before the ride, so book well in advance. Visit hh100.org for more information.

the Hotter'N Hell Hundred takes place. When temperatures regularly exceed 100°F, the wind blows hard and hot, and shade is an oh-so-precious resource.

But in 1982, when the city first decided to put on the Hotter'N Hell Hundred as part of a centennial celebration honoring the hardscrabble founders of Wichita Falls, they didn't have an idyllic bike ride in mind. They set out to create an event that would challenge even the fittest and most determined cyclists, honor the city's ancestors, and require the support of an entire community to pull off successfully.

Over its 3 decades of existence, the Hotter'N Hell Hundred has routinely shattered the morale of even pro racers, leaving them immobilized at the side of the road, clutching their cramp-seized hamstrings. The ride has fortified and buoyed an entire city, with a volunteer army made up of overwhelmingly hospitable locals.

Hotels book to capacity months in advance, and the university, Midwestern State, has become a collegiate cycling powerhouse, thanks to cycling scholarships made possible by the ride's proceeds. Today, the Hotter'N Hell Hundred is widely regarded across the United States as one of the most revered—and feared—century rides on earth.

Cyclists who attempt to complete the Hotter'N Hell Hundred risk severe dehydration, hallucinations, heart palpitations, and heat stroke. After hours of riding in record high temperatures (including 109°F in 2011) across hazy, sunbaked plains and into winds over 30 miles per hour, they finish without photos of mountaintop vistas or outstretched coastlines. But these finishers do recount intense memories from the barren roads surrounding Wichita Falls. The legendary themed rest stops, such as Margaritaville, where sorority co-eds sporting Hawaiian leis hand out fresh orange slices and pour ice-cold pitchers of blue Gatorade. The tenacious riders they met and swapped pulls with for hours, who then became lifelong friends. The disabled cyclists and wounded veterans they saw pedaling 100 miles using only hand cranks. The heavy finisher's medal that was draped around their neck, the sense of pride and accomplishment they felt, and the 32-ounce draft beers and giant smoked turkey legs they treated themselves to afterward.

As hundreds of thousands of Hotter'N Hell finishers can attest, sometimes you must ride out past the gates of hell to find your own little slice of heaven.

Interbike

NEVADA

Officially, Interbike, the largest bicycle trade show in North America, is an industry gathering where the makers and sellers of cycling products hawk their goods to bike shops and dealers. But since its inception in 1982, the event, held each fall in Las Vegas, has transformed into an annual celebration of the US bike industry. There's an outdoor mountain bike demo, held in Bootleg Canyon on 36 miles of International Mountain Bicycling Association (IMBA) Epic-designated cross-country and downhill trails. There's CrossVegas, which has become the biggest cyclocross race in America, drawing top European racers like former world champion Sven Nys. There's an assortment of celebrity cyclists and top professional racers posing for pictures and signing autographs. This is Vegas, after all, so of course there's booze and debauchery. And, amidst all the bike-related distractions, there's a giant exposition of insanely cool (sometimes ridiculously so) bike gear. It's at Interbike where companies unveil their innovative new products, each attempting to outdo the others by trotting out bikes and components specifically designed to pop eyes and attract attention. Interbike is where, if you're the kind of cyclist who lusts after the coolest new tech and salivates over beautiful bikes, you must go—and see for yourself.

Get There

▶▶ Interbike is technically for people employed within the cycling industry. So unless you produce or sell bike products or you're a member of the cycling media, you may have difficulty registering for Interbike. However, in recent years the event has increasingly opened its doors to everyday consumers. In 2014, Interbike hosted a customer appreciation day and sold tickets to the expo floor to the general public for $20. Visit interbike.com for more information.

Kingdom Trails

VERMONT

Up in the far corner of rural Vermont, a rugged landscape known as the Northeast Kingdom sits between the wide Connecticut River and the steep slopes of the Green Mountains. A wide web of more than 100 miles of trails spans this landscape, offering every type of off-road riding, from full-face-helmet-recommended downhill runs to all-day singletrack epics, as well as family- and beginner-friendly mountain bike loops. A full-time staff maintains and regularly upgrades the trail system, smoothing out sweeping berms, reinforcing the trails with stone embankments, and running wood ramps over sensitive trail sections. The unique network, called the Kingdom Trails, is managed as a nonprofit organization, partnering with more than 60 private landowners to provide mountain bike access. It will cost you to come ride these trails, but as the 60,000-plus people from around the world who annually visit the Kingdom Trails can attest, the flowing ride across the mountains of the Northeast Kingdom is well worth the price.

> ## Get There
>
> ▶▶ The Kingdom Trails Welcome Center, where staffers will provide you with a map and help you plan a route, is located in East Burke, Vermont. The quaint New England town is roughly a 2.5-hour drive from both Burlington, Vermont, and Montreal, Quebec. A day pass to access the Kingdom Trails is $15 and an annual pass is $75. Visit kingdomtrails.org for more information.

The Leadville 100

COLORADO

Bag a belt buckle at the Leadville 100. Back in the heyday of the Wild West, this town, the highest incorporated city in North America at 10,152 feet in elevation, bustled with both legitimate and nefarious activity. Miners dug holes into the mountainsides and extracted buckets full of silver, and an array of saloons, gambling halls, and brothels clambered to collect the treasure. Way up here in the high air of the Rocky Mountains, the Colorado town's population peaked at more than 30,000 people, and ornate brick buildings, including the historic Tabor Opera House, where Oscar Wilde once performed, soon lined the main strip, Harrison Avenue. In 1883, not long after his showdown at the O.K. Corral, the notorious dentist, gambler, and gunslinger Doc Holliday stumbled into town, broke and battling pneumonia. Soon, on the streets of Leadville, he found trouble again, in a confrontation with an ex-Leadville lawman over a $5 debt. Doc Holliday shot the man dead at the entrance of a saloon yet somehow managed to escape conviction by a local jury.

For decades, the entire populous of Leadville managed a similarly tenuous existence, reliant on the diminishing veins of silver or gold that ran through the 14,000-foot-tall peaks encircling the town. By the 1950s, the natural resources had been mostly exhausted. When the last major mining operation, the Climax Mine, stopped producing in the 1980s, Leadville faced two options: reinvent itself, or turn into a ghost town. Unwilling to watch his town shrivel up, in 1983 Ken Chlouber, a local miner and avid ultra runner, came up with the idea to hold a 100-mile running race out and back over Hope Pass, rising 12,500 feet above Leadville.

That first year, 45 runners showed up to race one another through the day and the night, trying to beat the 30-hour time limit to become an official finisher and earn a gleaming belt buckle at the end. The race, mostly due to its seeming insanity, gained international recognition and broadcast television coverage. Leadville transformed into an outdoor destination for the hardy and extreme athletes who prefer the rustic feel of the Old West to the glitzy resort towns like Aspen.

Eleven years after that first running race, Chlouber introduced a 100-mile mountain bike race, seizing on the booming popularity of the relatively new sport. Following a slightly different route, the mountain bike race climbed 3,126 feet up the exposed mountainside of Columbine Mine and across a treeless plateau surrounded by clouds—earning it the nickname "The Race Across the Sky." Mountain bikes remained relatively rudimentary at the time, and racing knobby tires over 100 miles on rugged jeep trails with nearly 14,000 feet of total elevation gain seemed ridiculous. That is exactly why the race started to take off.

Get There

▶▶ There are four ways to get into the Leadville Trail 100 MTB race: You need to be rich, fast, lucky, or charitable. The easiest method, with the least likelihood of success, is simply entering the online lottery by paying a $15 fee. Perhaps the hardest method, but potentially the most fun, is entering a Leadville 100 MTB qualifier, such as the Austin Rattler MTB at Rocky Hill Ranch just outside of Austin, Texas. Each Leadville qualifier race offers between 25 and 100 registration spots, selected from top age-group and overall finishers. The faster your finish in a Leadville qualifier race, the higher your start-line position in the Leadville 100 MTB. For those whose desire to participate in Leadville outweighs any financial concerns, there are three options: One is to participate in the Carmichael Training System's Camp of Champions, led by former multitime men's and women's Leadville 100 MTB winners Dave Wiens and Rebecca Rusch. The cost of participating in the camp is $750. The cost of participating in the camp with a guaranteed Leadville entry is $2,000. Or, entry to the Leadville MTB 100, along with a host of perks, is provided through the organization CEO Challenges for $1,900. Finally, a number of charitable organizations, including the Leadville Legacy Foundation and the Life Time Foundation, offer entry to the Leadville 100 MTB based on fund-raising goals. For more information, visit leadvilleraceseries.com.

By the mid-2000s, Leadville attracted many of the top American pro racers, and entry was limited to a lottery system that capped the participation at about 2,000 riders. In 2008, Lance Armstrong made headlines by losing the Leadville 100 to a local legend, Dave Wiens, a pro mountain biker who has won the race six times. The following year, amidst much hubbub, Armstrong returned with a documentary crew and crushed Wiens, along with the rest of the field, while setting a new course record of 6 hours and 28 minutes.

The Leadville 100 MTB race is generally credited with sparking the popularity of endurance mountain bike racing and the array of 100-mile off-road races across the country and around the world. Yet, Leadville, which Chlouber sold to the event promotions arm of Life Time Fitness in 2010, has also received criticism, in part based on its own popularity—there's now a series of qualifier events around the country at which racers can earn entry—and the cost of attending. A nonrefundable $15 fee is required to enter the lottery, and if you're lucky enough to make it into the event, there's a $345 registration fee.

Yet, no other race compares to Leadville in history and mystique, and sheer daunting challenge. Where else did Doc Holliday drunkenly wander the streets, revolver in hand? What other race starts with the crack of a shotgun at more than 10,000 feet in altitude and goes up from there? Is there a more coveted trophy than the plate-size belt buckle given to finishers who complete the grueling course in less than 12 hours? This town once teetered on the brink of ruin. Now it's become synonymous with the 100-mile mountain bike race across the crest of the Rockies, a race known to cyclists throughout the world as, simply, Leadville.

Maah Daah Hey

In the badlands of western North Dakota, a region defined by its barren, rippling hills, the Theodore Roosevelt National Park is divided into northern and southern segments. The Little Missouri National Grassland spans these two park segments, and the 97-mile Maah Daah Hey trail, within the Grassland, connects them. The Maah Daah Hey—almost entirely singletrack, save for the odd road or river crossing—zigzags through the Little Missouri River valley, traversing precipitous ridgelines, bypassing enigmatic rock formations, and crossing vast prairies. The trail is considered the longest continuous stretch of singletrack in the United States, and with its undulating terrain, complete lack of shade, and sparse water stops, it takes most riders multiple days to complete. The name, translated from the Native American Mandan dialect, means "an area that has been and will be here a long time." But the Maah Daah Hey isn't for everyone. A local outfitter, Dakota Cyclery, warns on its Web site, "Even if you're in top physical condition, riding a badlands trail will be extremely hard if not deadly." However, those who do ride the Maah Daah Hey from end to end can claim to have conquered the badlands by bike.

Get There

▶▶ The southern terminus of the Maah Daah Hey starts in Sully Creek State Park, near Medora, North Dakota. Dakota Cyclery in Medora offers shuttles, tours, and bike rentals (dakotacyclery.com). The Maah Daah Hey 100, held in early August, is a 100-mile race over the entire length of the trail. Visit experienceland.org for more information.

Moab

UTAH

For nearly as long as people have ridden bikes with knobby tires, those people have brought their bikes to this small town in eastern Utah, a rust-colored recreation paradise of sandstone canyons and high desert mountains on the banks of the Colorado River. Encircled by federally managed lands and situated at the cusp of the Arches and Canyonlands National Parks, Moab is perhaps most famous for its Slickrock trail, a completely unique experience that winds 10 miles through a lumpy expanse of Navajo sandstone. The route through the red-rock moonscape, situated on a plateau above town, is discernable only by the white dots spray-painted onto the stone and the line of tire marks left by the thousands of mountain bikers who've come here to ride across the roller-coaster-esque route.

But more and more, Moab is gaining acclaim for its singletrack trail systems expanding far beyond the Slickrock playground. There's Porcupine Rim, which traces a tall ledge overlooking the striking stone towers of Castle Valley and the bald peaks of the La Sal Mountains, which rise to 12,721 feet. There's the new Moab Brand Trails, accessible via the paved Moab Canyon bike path paralleling Highway 191, which offer everything from beginner-friendly double-track dirt roads to gnarly expert-only singletrack. And then there's the

Get There

▶▶ The closest city to Moab is Salt Lake City, 234 miles to the northwest. A number of bicycle shops offer top-end mountain bike rentals and shuttle service, including Poison Spider (poisonspiderbicycles.com), which runs shuttles daily to the drop-off point for the Whole Enchilada and offers guided day trips on the surrounding trails. Visit discovermoab.com for more information.

Whole Enchilada, Moab's most iconic off-road adventure. The epic ride, best accessed by shuttle from Moab, starts amidst the alpine slopes of the La Sal Mountains and drops 8,000 feet over 33 miles en route back to Moab, offering views that stretch as far as Colorado's San Juan Mountains and rocky, white-knuckle descents that will leave your arms shaking with fatigue and your mouth spread in a wide grin.

Moab certainly isn't the only tourism-based town to position itself as a hub of recreational activity and of mountain biking in particular. But it was one of the first to welcome mountain bikers to come ride the captivating landscape of the Southwest, and with the continued expansion of the trail system by local organizations like the recently formed Moab Mountain Bike Association, it's well positioned to remain one of the world's most-sought-out mountain biking destinations.

Mount Lemmon

ARIZONA

For many cyclists, the climb up Mount Lemmon starts at a coffee shop in a strip mall next to a Safeway. From here, the view is composed of acres of asphalt, completely contradicting the scenery and challenge of the mountain climb mere miles away. During every day of the week, and especially during Tucson's mild winters, Le Buzz Café teems with cyclists sipping espresso and filling up on freshly made baked goods before tackling the 27-mile ascent of Mount Lemmon.

Le Buzz Café sits at the southern terminus of the Catalina Highway, the singular road that rises from the suburban outskirts of Tucson toward the highest peak in the Santa Catalina Mountains. The official climb up Mount Lemmon starts at the intersection of Snyder Road and Catalina Highway (speed demons, hit your stopwatches here), but you won't truly feel like you're ascending a mountain until you hit the first perfectly rounded turn, about 1.5 miles

Get There

▶▶ Each May the Greater Arizona Bicycling Association puts on a supported ride up Mount Lemmon, with rest stops roughly every 6 miles offering fluids and healthy snacks. At the uppermost rest stop, the club serves freshly baked pies in honor of the beloved bakery in Summerhaven that once served weary cyclists but closed after a forest fire in 2003. Visit bikegaba.org for more information.

after the intersection. Rising at a consistent 5 percent in average gradient, the ride up Mount Lemmon proves challenging but not too challenging. For this reason, you'll spot cyclists ranging from retirees on hybrids to world-class professionals en route to the summit.

From the base to the peak, Mount Lemmon gains 6,000 feet in elevation, and the landscape shifts dramatically. As the road twists and turns along the various ridgelines leading to the top, you'll ride from the rocky, dry desert into a lush alpine forest with tall trees shading the road and the sound of gurgling brooks running down the mountain slope. It's nearly impossible to ride up Mount Lemmon for the first time without stopping for photo opportunities. During the winter, it's not uncommon to ride amongst banks of snow while overlooking the warm desert below. The rock spires that cling to the edges of Mount Lemmon, carved by time and weather into massive stone sculptures, seemingly defy the laws of physics.

At the 21-mile mark, the continuous climbing is given a respite as a brief descent leads to the mountaintop village of Summerhaven, where you'll find restaurants and shops at which to refuel. Many consider Summerhaven the summit of Mount Lemmon, but the road continues upward, climbing even more steeply to the Mount Lemmon Observatory and its cluster of round, white domes. From a rock ledge, you can look out over the rest of the Santa Catalina Mountains and toward Tucson, where just hours before you sat at the edge of a parking lot, sipping coffee.

Mount Tamalpais

CALIFORNIA

Escape to Mount Tamalpais. For cyclists trapped at the tip of the San Francisco Peninsula, only a few routes offer escape by bike. Luckily, the route across the Golden Gate Bridge, down into Sausalito, and up into the Marin foothills of Mount Tamalpais offers world-class riding. Climb up through the Muir Woods redwood forest on Shoreline Highway. Then, softly descend the grassy slopes on the other side until you're overlooking Muir Beach and spinning alongside the Pacific Ocean. A popular local route takes Fairfax-Bolinas Road, climbing 2,000-plus feet back up the hillside toward the summit of Mount Tamalpais. At the intersection of Ridgecrest Boulevard, you can either keep ascending toward the peak of Mount Tam, with its sweeping views of the Pacific coastline and the jagged Farallon Islands in the far-off distance, or roll back toward the city along Panoramic Highway, situated atop a precipitous crest with the surrounding hilltops spilling out to either side.

Get There

▶▶ Check in at Studio Velo in Mill Valley for local ride intel or to join one of the daily group rides heading up into the Marin hills. Finish your spin at the Gestalt Haus in Fairfax, where you can hang your bike on a wall hook and sit down to a giant brat and a local draft beer. Every September for more than half a century, the Golden Gate Velo cycling club has put on a hill-climb bike race up Mount Tam. The 12-mile-long race starts in Stinson Beach and is relatively flat for the first few miles before turning up Fairfax-Bolinas and Ridgecrest Roads. There's little prize money on the line, but for an entire year, the winner can claim they're the king of Mount Tam. Visit goldengatevelo.org for more information.

MOUNT TAMALPAIS

Mount Washington

NEW HAMPSHIRE

Atop this mountain, standing above the Presidential Range in the Appalachians of New Hampshire, the wind blows at hurricane force 100 days per year, once reaching a record wind speed of 231 miles per hour. There's nearly no vegetation up here, 6,288 feet in the air, just fields of granite boulders that stretch out so far locals refer to the mountaintop simply as the "rock pile." The Native Americans who once called this area home didn't dare come up here, such was their reverence for the gods whom they believed lived atop these peaks. But since as early as 1642, less-shrewd explorers have regularly ascended Mount Washington. In 1819, a bridle path was cut across the sheer face of the mountain, and in 1861, the path was transformed into a road. Today, the privately owned Mount Washington Auto Road is widely regarded as one of the steepest and most treacherous ascents in the United States. Over its 7.6-mile distance, the gradient averages 12 percent, with pitches that rise at grades of 22 percent. However, cyclists who come to conquer Mount Washington face more than just the length and vertical nature of the Auto Road. They also face the wind, which blows from all sides across the rock-strewn slopes of this mountain, a mountain that proudly claims to have the world's worst weather.

Get There

▶▶ Mount Washington is located 193 miles north of Boston. The Mount Washington Auto Road is accessible only by car or shuttle. However, twice a year you can race up the mountain with thousands of other cyclists during the Mount Washington Auto Road Bicycle Hillclimb and Newton's Revenge, held in August and July, respectively. Visit mtwashingtonautoroad.com for more information.

Natchez Trace Parkway

From the river bluffs of Natchez, Mississippi, to the Appalachian foothills of Nashville the Natchez Trace Parkway runs 444 miles through three states and 10,000 years of North American history. Built during the Great Depression as a public works project and designated a national park with a speed limit of 50 miles per hour, the parkway follows a route first forged by migrating buffalo and Native Americans and later used by Spanish explorers, British infantry, and early settlers of the southern United States. Today, numerous historic sites dot the Natchez Trace Parkway, including a ceremonial American Indian mound, Emerald Mound, and various sections of the original dirt path, sunk into the earth by thousands of travelers passing over the soft soil. However, for cyclists, the true draw of the Natchez Trace Parkway is the pure joy that riding the scenic road instills. The trace was worn along the path of least resistance, circling hills and bordering valleys, creating an ever-winding route through a landscape that remains nearly as rural as when the buffalo roamed here.

Get There

▶▶ If you plan on making a multiday trip along the Natchez Trace Parkway, the National Park Service maintains primitive campsites for touring cyclists at roughly 50-mile intervals. For more information on the history of the Natchez Trace, as well as attractions and accommodations along the route, visit the official National Park Service Web site at nps.gov/natr.

New York City and Environs

Ride a bike upon the bowed Williamsburg Bridge above the East River and you'll soon realize what so many New Yorkers adore about cycling in this big, complicated, beautiful city. Aboard a bike, you're no longer beholden to the paucity of parking spots, the exorbitant cab fares, the rat-infested subway tunnels. The turrets of the modern kingdom, Manhattan, splay out. Suddenly, you feel as if you own New York.

The world knows (and loves) New York for many things. But cycling? Let me explain. Over the past few years across the United States, numerous cities have made improvements for cyclists, but no municipality has done as much as quickly as New York. In 2008, powerful and moneyed naysayers scoffed when then mayor Michael Bloomberg unveiled an ambitious plan to transform New York's mean streets and reclaim them for people instead of cars. But look now: Gallons of green paint were spilled to create a citywide welcome zone for cyclists. There are 296 miles of new bike lanes, many of them barricaded from traffic by concrete and parking lanes, encouraging even casual cyclists to ride down Broadway and through a car-free Times Square. Flickering bicycle traffic lights usher packs of commuters across intersections. And 95,000 annual members subscribe to the nation's biggest bike share, Citi Bike. Look closely and you might even spot Leonardo DiCaprio or Seth Meyers pedaling one of the unmistakable blue bikes alongside you. Even Beyoncé's been known to commute to Brooklyn's Barclays Center by bike.

According to the US Census, more people, in total, get to work by bike in New York than anywhere else in the country. Storied bike cities like Boulder, Colorado, now come here to witness the vanguard in urban cycling. By 2020, current mayor Bill de Blasio vows, bikes will be the conveyances for 6 percent of all trips in the city.

In this metropolis of more than 8 million people, where fewer than half the residents own cars, cycling has long made sense. Congested streets and packed subways mean bikes are often the quickest method of travel from point A to B. But for decades, a car-oriented mind-set made high-quality bike lanes, paths, and bridges an afterthought. A hundred years ago, spectators packed Madison Square Garden to watch 6-day bicycle races. By the 1950s, the pastime had disappeared. A national infatuation with automobiles, along with the car-loving policies of highway baron Robert Moses, which categorized bicycles as toys rather than vehicles, nearly made cycling in NYC extinct. Only the brave or the desperate—messengers, deliverymen, and determined enthusiasts—dared to get around by bike.

But even as they choked on exhaust, New York's cycling advocates fought back. In 1973, they founded Transportation Alternatives and hailed the installation of protected bike lanes on Broadway and 6th Avenue in 1981 (though the lanes were torn out a month later, after mayor Ed Koch yielded to protesting cabbies). In 1987, advocates rallied the masses to defeat a bike ban in Midtown, and in 1991 cyclists finally gained access to the Queensboro Bridge after Transportation Alternatives members, including the organization's director, Jon Orcutt, blocked traffic with their bikes and welcomed arrest.

Get There

▸▸ Organizations such as Bike the Big Apple (bikethebigapple.com) offer guided bike tours of New York City. If you feel comfortable exploring on your own, grab a New York City bike map and pay $10 for a 24-hour Citi Bike rental. A variety of bike shops, such as Sid's (sidsbikes.com), offer high-end road bike rentals for adventures outside the city. Every May, more than 30,000 cyclists participate in the Five Boro Bike Tour, a 40-mile ride on traffic-free roads starting in Manhattan's Battery Park and finishing in Staten Island. Visit bike.nyc/events/td-five-boro-bike-tour for more information about the Five Boro Bike Tour, as well as route suggestions and advice on riding throughout the city.

But only after witnessing the transformations in quality of life—and the accompanying acclaim that followed—in bike-friendly international rivals like Paris and London did the city leaders truly begin to take cycling seriously. In 2008, a visionary and forceful transportation commissioner, Janette Sadik-Khan—who commuted by bike from the West Village to City Hall—set about reshaping New York into a city in which everyone could peacefully coexist. She hired Orcutt, the aforementioned advocate, as the policy director of the NYC Department of Transportation. In lieu of drawn-out planning studies, she installed experimental infrastructure using temporary paint and pylons. (When critical voices arose, she shot back, "It's just paint.")

Every August, Sadik-Khan closed 7 miles of Manhattan to cars and invited walkers, runners, cyclists, adults, children, even pets, to play on Park Avenue as part of an ongoing Summer Streets initiative. The open-streets festival won the hearts and minds of NYC residents. By the time Sadik-Khan left office in 2013, independent polls showed that 64 percent of New Yorkers supported bike lanes.

"There are 296 miles of new bike lanes, many of them barricaded from traffic by concrete and parking lanes, encouraging even casual cyclists to ride down Broadway and through a car-free Times Square."

Today, riding a bike in NYC is no longer an act of social protest. It's simply the fastest and most enjoyable way to get from point A (say, for example, Amy Ruth's chicken and waffles in Harlem) to point B (perhaps a dim sum feast in Chinatown). See for yourself by picking up a Citi Bike in Times Square and pedaling down a protected bike lane on Broadway to the farmer's market in Union Square, where you can sample apple wedges from upstate orchards. In Brooklyn, ride toward Greenpoint along Kent Avenue, a two-way protected bike lane demarcated by green paint, and stop at the Brooklyn Brewery for a tour and a tasting. Take the fully separated, tree-lined path running down the grassy median of Ocean Parkway from Prospect Park to Coney Island, where famous hot dogs, a long wooden boardwalk, and sandy beaches await.

Or ride one of the paths ringing Manhattan along the waterfront and wander away from the city. The Hudson River Greenway (New York's most beloved bike

THE BROOKLYN BRIDGE

trail) starts amidst Wall Street skyscrapers and runs north along the river, all the way to the fortress-like Cloisters museum at the tip of the island, where you can view one of the world's best collections of medieval art. To one side of the trail, the river gently laps against a rocky shoreline. To the other, families enjoy the manicured parks of the Upper West Side. The Greenway forks at the George Washington Bridge, and a winding climb rises to a dedicated path beside the bridge's busy traffic lanes. Crossing this massive, nearly 100-year-old steel structure rivals any bridge crossing, anywhere. To the west, the towering, sheer rock face of the Palisades rises over 300 feet above the Hudson and stretches 20 miles north up the river. To the east, the stunning Manhattan skyline comes fully into view.

Where the bridge's cycling path terminates in Fort Lee, New Jersey, a mesmerizing park road, Henry Hudson Drive, leads cyclists 8 miles alongside the Palisades, past waterfalls streaming down the cliff face, and up a 1-mile-long climb to Route 9W, a veritable cycling highway with its wide shoulders and packs of riders pedaling toward the quaint Hudson Valley towns of Piermont and Nyack.

As in all major cities, cycling in New York still requires plenty of caution. But the initiative Vision Zero aims to declaw the lingering culture of roadway lawlessness. The program, which originated in Sweden, has dropped speed limits to 25 miles per hour across the city and increased ticketing for reckless driving. The safer streets and influx of new cyclists in New York has led to a revival of the widespread bike culture last seen during the track racing heyday of the early 1900s.

Take the Red Hook Criterium, where dozens of fit men and women race track bikes—which neither coast nor brake—around the Brooklyn Cruise Terminal at night. Racers and industry reps come from as far as Montreal and Italy for the race, and around the entirety of the circuitous course, fans line the railing 10 deep. The crowds that once filled the garden for 6-day races have been reborn a century later in Red Hook. The race captures the zeitgeist of the urban cycling movement and intrigues both utilitarian cyclists and hard-core bike racers. But it's more than just the race that makes this evening so unique. It's something more ephemeral in the scene and the setting; the styles on display, the buildings surrounding this centuries-old shipping terminal, the lights reflecting on the water. Simply put, it's New York.

Old Fall River Road

COLORADO

This route, first carved by glaciers, then cut into a trail by Native American hunters, and finally made into a roadway by convicts equipped with nothing more than hand tools, rises toward the Continental Divide within the confines of Colorado's Rocky Mountain National Park. Started in 1913 and not completed until 1920, Old Fall River Road follows the contours of the wide Fall River Valley, ascending more than 3,000 feet over 11 miles into the heart of the Rocky Mountains. On this single-lane dirt road, you'll ride past rushing waterfalls, wild bighorn sheep, and herds of grazing elk. You'll climb high above the tree line and wind your way up switchbacks overlooking shimmering glacial ponds. At the summit, at an elevation of 11,796 feet, you'll find the Rocky Mountain National Park's Alpine Visitor Center and the intersection of Trail Ridge Road. Built just 12 years after the completion of Old Fall Road, in 1932, the more-visited Trail Ridge Road is the highest continuously paved roadway in the United States and provides a 24-mile descent across windswept ridgelines back toward the town of Estes Park.

Get There

▶▶ Old Fall River Road starts 7 miles west of Estes Park. The daily entrance fee for cyclists to Rocky Mountain National Park is $10. The road is closed during the winter and free of car traffic for a brief period each spring when it is open to just cyclists and hikers. Visit nps.gov/romo for more information.

The Old Spokes Home

VERMONT

Step back in time at the Old Spokes Home. In Burlington, Vermont, at the northern edge of town, not far from the windswept waters of icy Lake Champlain, sits a small bike shop with a gravel parking lot and a tin roof. To one side of the bike shop is a store that deals strictly in junk, its name, Junktiques, scrawled on a metal garbage can hanging over the front door. On the other side, there's a garage, Champlain Transmission. The bike shop is called the Old Spokes Home, and a sign near the street rightfully declares, USED BIKES, BOUGHT, SOLD AND TRADED.

If you've ever had a bike shop that you loved, where you knew the employees by name or maybe cracked a beer in the parking lot after a twilight mountain bike ride, then seeing the Old Spokes Home from this vantage point, you'd likely discern that there's something special inside, that this shop has stories. Some unknown gravitational force would draw you through the doors, and you'd quickly notice that although the shop is bustling with customers, there are few fancy road bikes and little in carbon fiber on display. Rather, sturdy metal frames, thick rubber tires, and an expansive assortment of racks, baskets, and fenders adorn the shop floor—these, the tools of urban and exurban bicycle adventurers.

As the name suggests, the Old Spokes Home occupies a certain niche amongst the pantheon of great bike shops, specifically, old bikes. From the ceilings and along the shop's walls hang antique bikes, some of them more than 100 years old. But these aren't just cool old bikes. Each bike at the Old Spokes Home tells a certain tale in the evolution of the world's most efficient vehicle, the bicycle, as well as a much broader ongoing narrative about human mobility. To hear the story in full, you must seek out the genial owner of the Old Spokes Home, the thickly bearded man with the cap pulled low on his forehead, Glenn Eames.

Shake Eames's hand and ask to see the bicycle museum. Tell him that you've seen it online or read about it in magazines and books. Follow him through a door and up a narrow flight of stairs into an expansive attic with exposed wooden rafters. Here is the Old Spokes Home's private museum, the thing that distinguishes this shop, that you may have surmised exists. The bicycles hang from ropes tied to the ceiling and stand in mounts specially fabricated to accommodate their unconventional wheels. Plaques bearing each bike's name and a short description adorn a wooden railing.

Like a chapter in a book, every item in Eames's carefully selected collection of 70 or so two-wheeled artifacts serves a specific purpose in telling the story of the bicycle. Eames, both the curator and docent of this collection, is most concerned with a specific time period in the history of the bicycle, from the end of the Civil War to the beginning of the 1900s, an era predating widespread use of the internal combustion engine. During this period the bicycle proved most transformative in improving personal mobility. Where a trip of 100 miles might have taken multiple days by horseback or carriage, in the 1870s cyclists on high-wheeled bicycles often completed such journeys before sunset.

The museum's story begins with the Calvin Whitty velocipede of 1868, a serpentine-style iron frame draped over two radially spoked wood wheels of similar size, with the crank arms attached to the front wheel. The

> ## Get There
>
> ▶▶ The Old Spokes Home is located at 322 North Winooski Avenue, Burlington, Vermont. The museum is open during shop hours. Visit oldspokeshome.com for more information and to view the online gallery of historic bikes.

museum features more than half a dozen of these velocipedes (the machine predated the term "bicycle"), with each signifying a particular advancement in bicycle technology. Ornately crafted by carriage makers of the era, the velocipedes' leather saddles sit aloft bouncy leaf springs, an effort to ease the jarring effect of the stiff wooden spokes that gave early velocipedes the nickname boneshakers.

Because the design of the velocipede limited the speed at which it could travel to the size of the front wheel, front wheels soon got larger and larger. Eventually, only the length of the rider's legs limited the bike's gearing. The style was known as an "ordinary" (in comparison with later bicycle designs) and a "penny farthing" (for the disparate sizes of the British coins, the penny and the farthing), but it's perhaps most recognizable to those unfamiliar with antique bicycles as the "high wheeler," having a massive front wheel and tiny rear wheel. Nearly a dozen high wheelers sit on display at the Old Spokes Home, and Eames himself once rode a century on one of these, a 52-inch-wheeled model.

The beauty of the high wheeler was its speed; a bike similar to the Old Spokes Home's J.I. Stassen "Nonpareil" (meaning "without equal") from 1873 was one of the first high wheelers ever made, and it featured a 4.5-foot-tall front wheel. It was ridden from Bath to London, 108 miles, in 8 hours, at that time an unimaginable pace. The downfall of the high wheeler was, well, the downfall. A simple rock or pothole could cause a cyclist speeding along with glee to be flung over the front wheel and slammed headfirst into the ground in the dreaded "header." High wheel cyclists frequently died from such incidents.

The bicycles that followed the high wheeler aimed to correct this deadly problem, and they're prominently displayed at the Old Spokes Home, too. The museum's Xtraordinary Challenge, made by famed sewing machine company Singer, and the Facile (both built in 1884) used levered crank arms to position the rider farther behind the front wheel, lessening the risk of tipping forward. Then in the 1890s came the safety bicycle. With the safety bicycle, the evolution of the bicycle both ends and begins. The double-diamond frame and the geared rear wheel have remained the standard for nearly all bicycles for more than 100 years.

Yet, where major evolutionary changes in the basic design of the bicycle ceased, innovations in speed, comfort, and utility continued at a rapid pace. The Old Spokes Home documents all of this, as well. There's the 1893 Columbia Model 32, with its huge, heavily sprung saddle, its elliptical chainring, pneumatic tires, and rear drum brake. There's Old Hickory (one of two wooden bicycles on display), made in 1897 from layers of laminated hickory curved into frame tubes, chainstays, and a front fork and held together with ornate metal lugs.

There's an array of chainless bicycles, including the King Chainless, a likely prototype built prior to 1897 that used a rigid drive rod to power the rear wheel and featured a geared transmission box below the bottom bracket. A bright yellow Model

M chainless made by E.C. Stearns from Syracuse, New York in 1899, with its drive-shaft housed inside the chainstay, is nearly identical to a version used by the era's greatest racer, Major Taylor, to break world records.

There are tandems: a three-person tandem used to pace track racers in training sessions before motorized scooters were around to perform such a task and an Iver Johnson tandem, built in Massachusetts in 1898 with a linkage system between the front and rear handlebars, allowing both riders to steer the bike.

Though Eames bought many of the bikes in his collection in the kind of shape you might expect a 100-year-old bike to be in—with disintegrating tires and cracked leather seats, rusted steel frames and moldy wooden rims—almost every bicycle at the Old Spokes Home is restored to near-original condition. Along with the bicycles, Eames acquired the antique tools needed to work on them. He's reverse-engineered how some of the innovative gearing systems worked. He's even custom-manufactured specific parts needed to return some bikes to working order.

All of this care and attention, all the hours, all the money Eames has poured into this museum have been done with the intention of illustrating the story he's trying to tell. In the early 19th century, the Industrial Revolution quickly eclipsed the momentum of the bicycle, turning the developed world's focus to fossil fuel–powered movement and away from human-powered movement. But now, with the warming of our Earth, the depletion of our natural resources, and the growth of our midsections, we're realizing that while automobiles are incredible vehicles, they're also costly.

"The bicycle transports you from point A to B, and it pays you back," Eames says. Today, around the world, cities are re-embracing the bicycle and widely championing the environmental, financial, physical, and mental health benefits of riding. Eames says 100 years ago, advertising testimonials for bicycles touted similar benefits, including the sense of connection to the outdoors a bicycle gives its rider. One day soon, Eames says, we may look back on the 20th-century rise of automobiles as a skip on the record of human mobility.

Lest we ever forget the many blessings the bicycle has brought us, a trip to the northern edge of Burlington near the windswept water of Lake Champlain, up the narrow staircase at the back of the shop, and into the attic with the exposed wooden rafters will quickly help us remember.

RAGBRAI

IOWA

Welcome to Mount Vernon, Iowa, located in the rolling hills 15 miles west of Cedar Rapids. On pretty much any day of the year, arriving in Mount Vernon on First Street Northwest provides a relatively tranquil experience. The surrounding farmland morphs into a tall canopy of shady oak trees. At the historic Cornell College on the eastern edge of town, students walk across a grassy mall, past stately redbrick buildings. Women in sundresses mill around the street-front clothing boutiques, galleries, and cafes in the town center. It's a pastoral setting, Mayberry reborn on the banks of the Cedar River.

Then, there's the scene every few years when RAGBRAI arrives in Mount Vernon. RAGBRAI, the Register's Annual Great Bicycle Ride Across Iowa, started in 1973 when two *Des Moines Register* newspaper writers decided to ride across the state with a few hundred friends. During its over 40 consecutive years in existence, the 7-day, over-400-mile tour from the Nebraska state line to the Illinois state line (the Missouri River to the Mississippi) has grown into one of the world's biggest such cycling events. Today, more than 10,000 riders pedal 50 to 100 miles a day across the Hawkeye State, bringing a rolling party to every little town along the route.

In 2012, a local planning committee began preparing months in advance of RAGBRAI's passing through Mount Vernon. They coordinated various food vendors, set up a live music venue, and encouraged residents to dress in costumes representing the official theme, "Get Funky in Mount Vernon," and line up along First Street to enthusiastically welcome RAGBRAI riders to their town.

By 6:00 a.m. on the day of the RAGBRAI arrival, a handful of riders had already made it to Mount Vernon from the overnight stop in Cedar Rapids. By 9:00 a.m., the pubs along Front Street had opened their doors, and a sports bar prominently advertised Long Island Iced Teas, Jell-O shots, and an outdoor beer garden. By 10:00 a.m., thousands of RAGBRAI riders had flooded the town center. In between live sets from the Lincoln Highway Band, a DJ blared Pink's party anthem, "Raise Your Glass" (a song, fittingly, about letting go of your social inhibitions and just having fun). Riders put their gloved hands in the air, kicked up their bike-shoe-clad feet, and shook their spandex-bedecked butts. A middle-aged couple danced like a pair of horny teenagers on top of a picnic table. A woman dressed in a neon tank top twirled a Hula-Hoop around her hips, and a bare-chested man randomly flexed his pecks. When Pink dropped the chorus ("RAISE . . . YOUR . . . GLASS!") everyone started jumping up and down, thrusting their water bottles and beer cans into the air.

But it wasn't all electrolyte-mix-and-alcohol-fueled mayhem in Mount Vernon on the morning RAGBRAI arrived. Up the street, at the First Presbyterian Church, riders chowed down on rhubarb pie and (true story) rhubarb sausage. Across the street, below the tall stone steeple of the First Methodist Church, volunteers sold boiled eggs and homemade granola bars. At an abandoned gas station on the way into town, the Mount Vernon Fine Arts Association aimed to sell 8,500 freshly

> **" By 9:00 a.m., the pubs had opened their doors, and a sports bar prominently advertised Long Island Iced Teas, Jell-O shots, and an outdoor beer garden. "**

cooked breakfast burritos. The money would fund a high school trip to New York. James Kennedy, a well-known local guitarist, performed his blend of jazz, Latin, and rock fusion on the grassy lawn of his home, right on the RAGBRAI route.

As an official RAGBRAI meeting point, the retrofitted school buses that teams of riders use to haul their gear and provide support during the ride were steered toward the parking lot at Cornell College. These buses are as much a part of RAGBRAI as the actual riding. Step aboard the bus of Team Jorts—a perennial RAGBRAI favorite whose members ride in denim-colored cycling shorts and sleeveless jerseys that look like tuxedo tops—and you'll find a lounge area, refrigerator, fully stocked wet bar, and bathroom. Atop the bus, which is painted black with the bright Team Jorts logo prominently painted across the side, there's a wooden deck that doubles as a bike rack and a pre-, mid-, and post-ride party zone.

Get There

▶▶ The RAGBRAI route varies each year, with host and pass-through towns selected via an application process, but always travels west to east to take advantage of prevailing winds. Entry is limited to 8,500 weeklong riders and 1,500 day riders. In some years the event sells out, in which case entries are subject to a lottery. Riders are allowed to place one bag weighing up to 50 pounds on the semi truck that follows the ride. A number of sanctioned charter services offer amenities such as luggage storage, showers, tent setup, and even airport pickup and drop-off. Visit ragbrai.com for more information.

On the way out of Mount Vernon, headed toward the next small town—and the next live music show, homemade pie vendor, freshly grilled pork chop purveyor—RAGBRAI riders returned to quiet roads undulating through fields of corn. Farmers strung rolls of toilet paper in front of the tall green stalks, welcoming riders to, um, fertilize their crops. Children set up lemonade stands and stood in their gravel driveways spraying garden hoses, offering a brief respite from the late-July heat. A cardboard sign read 100-FOOT WATERSLIDE, with an arrow that pointed the way.

Eventually, the last of the RAGBRAI riders pedaled away from Mount Vernon, collectively leaving behind hundreds of thousands in tourism dollars. Every year, RAGBRAI brings a warmly received economic stimulus (totaling in the millions) to the rural communities it visits. The ride truly does help high school kids go on life-changing trips. It raises money for veterans and cancer research and hundreds of other important charities. It exposes the 50 percent of riders who come from outside the state (and otherwise might not put Iowa on their list of vacation destinations) to the genuine warmth, hospitality, and friendliness of the Midwest.

"Iowa nice" is a term regularly used on RAGBRAI.

With RAGBRAI gone, Mount Vernon returned to its usual tranquil self—but knowing that one day soon, the world's oldest, largest, and longest recreational bicycle touring event would return, and on that day, Mount Vernon would be ready.

Route of the Hiawatha

IDAHO

A century ago, fierce competition led railroad companies to forge increasingly audacious and expensive routes. In an effort to carve out new territory, the lines pushed west, through rugged, mountainous terrain previously considered impassable.

In the late 1800s, the Milwaukee Road company began planning one such route across the thickly forested Bitterroot Mountains in the Idaho Panhandle. Between 1906 and 1911, more than 6,000 men, mostly European immigrants, worked year-round, even in harsh weather, to construct the rail line, at a cost of $243 million.

Upon its completion, the new line between Chicago and the Pacific Northwest was deemed one of the most scenic stretches of railroad in North America. The most-storied passenger train to run the line, the Olympian Hiawatha, operated from 1947 to 1961. But by the 1980s, train travel had fallen from favor, and the route was abandoned. Rail enthusiasts lamented the loss, but cyclists saw an opportunity.

Get There

▶▶ The Route of the Hiawatha is managed by the Lookout Pass Ski and Recreation Area, located midway between Spokane, Washington, and Missoula, Montana, just off Interstate 90 at exit 0. Check in at Lookout Pass to purchase tickets, rent bikes, and reserve seats on the shuttle at the western terminus of the trail if you choose not to ride the gentle grade back up to the eastern trailhead. You can also purchase tickets to the Route of the Hiawatha from trail rangers along the way. Visit ridethehiawatha.com for more information.

A decade later, as the rails-to-trails movement swept across the country, the conversion of the rail line, dubbed the Route of the Hiawatha, became a marquee project. Opened to the public in 1998, the 15-mile trail features 10 tunnels carved from the mountainsides and 7 trestles spanning deep valleys of tall pine trees. At the eastern trailhead, on the border between Idaho and Montana, cyclists begin or finish their ride by passing through the 1.6-mile-long Taft Tunnel.

From the eastern trailhead, the Route of the Hiawatha descends at a gradual 2 percent gradient, making the ride an all-abilities experience. You'll spot packs of families, from grandparents to toddlers, taking in the Bitterroot Mountains by bike.

> **Between 1906 and 1911, more than 6,000 men, mostly European immigrants, worked year-round to construct the rail line, at a cost of $243 million.**

San Juan Hut Systems

COLORADO

There's a trail, 215 miles long, linking the high Rocky Mountains of Durango, Colorado, with the desert canyons of Moab, Utah, two of the most celebrated mountain biking locales in the United States. The route, a mixture of little-used forest roads and flowing singletrack, passes through a wilderness of five different national forests, across valleys of pine and aspen, and atop rocky ridgelines that bring the entirety of this mountainous scenery into view. And, thanks to a chain of fully stocked cabins roughly 30 miles apart, you can spend 7 days and 6 nights riding across this landscape with little more than a loaded CamelBak.

Known as the San Juan Hut Systems, the wood cabins were built by hand by an avid cross-country skier and mountain biker, Joe Kelly, and opened in 1987. The huts sleep eight people on padded bunks with sleeping bags, have wood-burning fireplaces, and come stocked with enough food for three full meals, including burritos, bacon and eggs, and, naturally, cold beer. All of this allows you to climb and descend through the Rocky Mountain backcountry without the burden of a heavy load, and with a grin across your face from ear to ear.

Get There

▸▸ The 6-day, 7-night San Juan Hut Systems trip costs $895 per person, with discounts for groups of four and eight that bring the cost down to $671 per person. A variety of shuttle services offer transportation back to Durango from Moab or will shuttle your car from Durango to Moab. Download the "Biker's Bible" at sanjuanhuts.com for more information about trip logistics, safety, and liability.

San Juan Islands

WASHINGTON

An observation tower built from stone and timber stands atop Mount Constitution, located on Washington State's Orcas Island, 2,409 feet above the surrounding Salish Sea. Modeled after the medieval watchtowers of Europe's Caucasus Mountains, the Civilian Conservation Corps built this imposing structure in 1936, originally as a fire lookout. Today, if you make the 4.7-mile ascent from the gates of Moran State Park, within which Mount Constitution sits, and climb the switchbacks that rise steeply through a canopy of tall green pines, you'll reap the reward of walking up the wooden stairs to the tower's observation deck, with its 360-degree views stretching out across the surrounding San Juan Islands, British Columbia, and, on clear days, the snowcapped peak of Mount Baker, standing 10,781 feet high amidst Washington's Northern Cascade Mountains.

The view from atop Mount Constitution may prove inspiring, but it's simply one of many highlights for those who cycle the San Juan Islands. On Lopez Island, the first stop on the 45-minute ferry ride from the coastal town of Anacortes, you'll pedal mild terrain and past friendly locals who have a habit of waving at any passerby, bicyclist, driver, or pedestrian. On San Juan Island, the namesake and largest of the archipelago's 172 different isles, you'll ride through vineyards and lavender farms, past

> ### Get There
>
> ▶▶ The Anacortes Ferry Terminal is located 81 miles north of Seattle. Interisland ferry travel is free by foot or bicycle. Bicycle rentals are available on San Juan, Lopez, and Orcas Islands. Go to visitsanjuans.com for more information.

lighthouses fronting the rocky shore. You'll stop to explore the San Juan Island National Historical Park and read the documentation of the nonviolent battle, known as the Pig War, between the British and Americans for control of the islands. You'll dine at cafés serving seafood pulled from the water that day and visit galleries featuring works by the local artisans who've come to inhabit these islands. You'll spot whales, surely, and you'll never face a ride that's too long or too challenging—that is, until you take on the climb to the watchtower atop Mount Constitution on Orcas Island.

SAN JUAN ISLAND

Skyline Drive

VIRGINIA

Across the country, a road that runs along the ridges of a chain of mountains or hills is frequently referred to as a skyline drive. The reason, of course, is that traveling the roadway engenders a certain atmospheric feeling, with views to either side of mountains and valleys stretching toward the horizon.

In 1931, at the start of the Great Depression, the Works Progress Administration began building a road that follows the ridgeline of the Appalachian Mountains, rising from the floor of the Shenandoah Valley. The construction, both difficult and dangerous, required workers to slice away sheer rock faces and tunnel through mountain peaks. The road was finally completed in 1939, and the resulting 105 miles of pavement connecting Front Royal, Virginia, with Waynesboro is widely considered the quintessential skyline drive, worldwide.

The entirety of Skyline Drive resides within Shenandoah National Park, where the speed limit is a pedestrian 35 miles per hour. The road weaves through tunnels of old-growth forest bursting with autumn colors in mid-to-late October and sweeps past the solid stone retaining walls of more than 70 scenic overlooks—where, the legend goes, if you squint hard enough, you can see the nation's capital, 69 miles away.

> ## Get There
>
> ▶▶ Skyline Drive starts in Front Royal, Virginia, 75 miles west of Washington, DC, and ends 105 miles later in Waynesboro, Virginia. The road continues south as the Blue Ridge Parkway. The entrance fee for a bicycle is $8 from March through November and $5 from December through February. Visit nps.gov/shen for more information.

Riding Skyline Drive requires fitness and skill, as the road slopes either up or down, never lying flat, and the first 5 miles, rising from Front Royal to the ridgeline, climb nearly 2,000 feet. But cyclists who take on the challenge will ride alongside soaring bald eagles and amongst wispy white clouds. They may spot a black bear, or more, and meet Appalachian Trail through-hikers where the trail parallels the roadway.

After riding Skyline Drive through the Shenandoah National Park, all those other scenic "skyline drives" will seem utterly inferior.

"The road weaves through tunnels of old growth forest bursting with autumn colors in mid-to-late October and sweeps past the solid stone retaining walls of more than 70 scenic overlooks—where, the legend goes, if you squint hard enough, you can see the nation's capital, 69 miles away."

Terlingua

TEXAS

Deep in the dusty shoehorn of Texas, if you don't miss it, you'll find a town—a ghost town, the handful of locals proudly pronounce—where striated mountains rise from the banks of the Rio Grande and the nighttime stars truly do beam brighter, where the quicksilver mines—the sole reason anyone inhabited this barren landscape in the first place, dried up a century ago—left behind a rocky graveyard of weathered wooden crosses, and where a stuffed billy goat, a former mayor, stands on display at the sole merchant's establishment. In this town, Terlingua, the land that land prospectors once dubbed "the final frontier," you'll find roads and trails, scenery and people (people baked dark by the desert sun, and here, welcomed with all their eccentricities), unlike anywhere else.

Terlingua sits between two giant parks, the Big Bend National Park and the Big Bend Ranch State Park. The national park offers rides such as the Old Ore Road, which traverses 30 miles of cactus-laden desert through gravely arroyos and past towering mesas, and culminates with an offer of a dip in an ancient hot spring, across the river from the tiny Mexican village of Boquillas. Roadies can tackle the park's 5-mile climb up Chisos Basin Road, where Emory Peak overlooks the Rio Grande Valley.

In the state park, just west of Terlingua, more than 100 miles of trails encircle rock domes and slice through painted canyon walls. The best-known (and most-feared)

> **Get There**
>
> ▸▸ Terlingua is a 5.5-hour drive from the nearest major city, El Paso. To avoid searing midday heat, plan your trip between September and May. The Chihuahuan Desert Bike Fest takes place each February and draws hundreds of riders. Visit desertsportstx.com for more information.

ride, the 55-mile Fresno-Sauceda Loop, has been designated an IMBA Epic. The almost entirely singletrack loop spans the more than 300,000-acre park from top to bottom. Pros knock the ride out in under 5 hours. Saner riders take 2 days, overnighting midway at the park's well-equipped Sauceda Ranch House.

"The undulating 46-mile road, El Camino del Rio (River Road) seems stolen from the screen of an old Western movie."

State park staff advise riders to start the Epic with at least 100 ounces of water and caution against making the journey alone, for there are few places a person can ride a bike that feel (and actually are) more isolated than Big Bend. When you arrive at the jagged rock outcroppings that rise 1,000 feet from the desert floor, layered upon one another like rows of shark teeth, you've reached the collapsed dome of an ancient volcano, the Solitario (in English: "solitary"). Somewhere out there in the Solitario, it's said, a tiny bar stands, most often unmanned, cobbled together from weathered boards. At the Solitario Bar, bikers can lay down their packs, kick up their feet, and, if they're lucky, enjoy a refreshment in return for a small donation.

The paved route through the state park and along the United States–Mexico border connects the upscale resort of Lajitas with the ruins of historic Fort Leaton in Presidio. The undulating 46-mile road, El Camino del Rio ("River Road"), seems stolen from the screen of an old Western movie (and has been featured in a number of films and TV series). On River Road, the panorama of scenic foliage and terrain includes 60 different species of cactus, from ocotillo to yucca; the odd grove of cottonwoods rising from the river; bright yellow and red desert flowers; and mountains perpetually transformed by the protracted shadows that shift across their faces.

At the end of each day, return to Terlingua, to the porch of the Trading Company, facing east. Grab a beer and a chair next to the assortment of fellow travelers and local desert people, the latter identifiable by their weathered looks and affable demeanor. Gaze into the distance, toward the Chisos Mountains, and enjoy the show as the setting sun turns the distant rocks golden, then pink, then deep, dark red.

TransAmerica Bicycle Trail

OREGON TO VIRGINIA

A number of excellent routes will get you across the United States by bike: You can ride beside waves breaking on the Pacific coast along US Highway 101; on back roads paralleling Interstate 10, from the canyon lands of the Southwest through New Orleans to the Florida beaches; or follow the historic Underground Railroad (see page 178) from the deep south through the Midwest, into Canada. But only one route, the TransAmerica Bicycle Trail, is recognized as the first official bicycle route across the United States, and it remains the most popular way to ride across the country.

In 1976, an event called the Bikecentennial, organized by a handful of youthful cycling enthusiasts, captivated the imaginations of bike riders across the United States and around the world. In celebration of the nation's 200th anniversary, more than 4,000 people (200 of them from Holland alone) embarked on group-led tours across America. These early cycling adventurers relied on the hospitality offered in small towns along the route, eating at local churches, showering in school gymnasiums, and sleeping in farmers' fields. They forged the route, from sea to shining sea, that thousands of people embark upon each year. The Bikecentennial organization eventually became the Adventure

> ## Get There
>
> ▶▶ Plan on taking roughly 3 months to bike across the United States, a 4,232-mile journey. The Adventure Cycling Association (adventurecycling.org) provides detailed water- and sweat-resistant maps of the route. The truly hard-core might consider participating in the Trans Am Bike Race, a self-supported ultra-endurance race across the United States that follows the TransAmerica Trail.

Cycling Association, which helps manage and advocate for the TransAmerica Bicycle Trail.

The trail starts in Astoria, Oregon, and ends in Yorktown, Virginia (or vice versa), avoiding major roadways as well as the southwestern deserts and taking in a vast array of scenery across the Rockies, Ozarks, Appalachians, and Great Plains and along portions of both the western and eastern seaboards. Major attractions include Yellowstone National Park, Civil War sites in Missouri, and the early colonial settlement of Williamsburg, Virginia.

> **Ask anyone who's ridden the TransAmerica Trail and they'll tell you it's the unexpected encounters they remember the most, the people they met along the route that made them realize that we Americans are far more alike than we are divided.**

The communities that somewhat warily welcomed the strange sight of thousands of tourists riding across the country during the Bikecentennial have come to form a bike-friendly industry around the route. There's Cooky's Café in Golden City, Missouri, known for the best slice of pie on the trail, and Newton Bike Shop in Newton, Kansas, which provides cross-country cyclists with overnight lodging—including a full-service kitchen, bike wash, and repair station—for just $10 a night.

A ride across the United States will undoubtedly include the grand and the glorious, the America of our geography textbooks and history classes. But ask anyone who's ridden the TransAmerica Trail and they'll tell you it's the unexpected encounters they remember the most, the roadside markers they read, the spur trails they explored, the people they met along the route, that made them realize that we Americans are far more alike than we are divided. The common refrain of those who've ridden the TransAmerica Trail is that they learned more about our country in 90 days of bicycling than most people do in a lifetime.

TRANSAMERICA
BICYCLE TRAIL

The Underground Railroad
Bicycle Route

The Yankee abolitionist showed Jacob Cummings the Ohio River on a map. He told Cummings how it separated slave states like Kentucky and Tennessee from free states like Indiana. The abolitionist urged Cummings to cross the river, then continue northward, toward Canada. He pointed out the Little Dipper and how it looked like a drinking gourd and the North Star at the tip of the gourd's handle. It would help guide him.

Cummings escaped a hard master in Chattanooga, Tennessee, and followed the star on foot for some 300 miles, until he found himself at the bank of the Ohio River. By the light of the moon he traversed the water's edge, eventually finding a small skiff chained to a tree. He hammered at the lock with a rock until it broke, then climbed into the boat and started paddling—toward freedom.

Some 150 years later, the path Cummings walked beside the Ohio River has become part of the Underground Railroad Bicycle Route (UGRR), which retraces the daring escapes of thousands of slaves and the brave individuals who assisted them. The entire route spans the continent, from Mobile, Alabama, where little history of abolitionist activity exists because anyone who aided slaves cautiously destroyed the evidence, to Owen Sound, Ontario, a community established by the freedom seekers who succeeded in reaching Canada. For bicycle tourists and history buffs without the ability to take on the full 2,006-mile journey, the 263-mile section through the Ohio River Valley from Louisville to Cincinnati features wonderfully narrow roads winding along the ridges above the Ohio's banks, as well as a concentration of historic Underground Railroad sites. This area, which includes the intersections of Indiana, Ohio, and Kentucky, was referred to as the Borderland due to the frequent pre–Civil War conflicts along this portion of the Ohio River.

There are many routes catering to cross-country cyclists—along the coasts, through the Rockies or Appalachians, across the midwestern farmland or the southwestern desert—but only the UGRR combines a cross-continental bicycle journey with such an important and dramatic period in our nation's history. To designate a single route representing the thousands taken by slaves fleeing northward, the Adventure Cycling Association mapped a course outlined by the folk slave song "Follow the Drinking Gourd."

When the Sun comes back
And the first quail calls,
Follow the Drinking Gourd.
For the old man is a-waiting for to carry you to freedom
If you follow the Drinking Gourd.

The riverbank makes a very good road.
The dead trees will show you the way.
Left foot, peg foot, traveling on,
Follow the Drinking Gourd.

The river ends between two hills,
Follow the Drinking Gourd.
There's another river on the other side,
Follow the Drinking Gourd.

When the great big river meets the little river,
Follow the Drinking Gourd.
For the old man is a-waiting for to carry you to freedom
If you follow the Drinking Gourd.

The lyrics of the song contain secret instructions to guide freedom-seeking slaves on their journeys. As Cummings wandered the northern bank of the Ohio, it's possible he recited this very song until he arrived in New Albany, Indiana. This city, situated directly across the river from Louisville served as an important first stop along the Underground Railroad for fugitive slaves escaping the barges bound for Southern plantations down river.

In 1850, as an effort to ease tensions between Borderland states and cities such as New Albany and Louisville, the US Congress passed the Fugitive Slave Act. The law made it illegal to aid fugitive slaves, but many were undeterred. In New Albany, Cummings found shelter with members of the free black community.

As you leave New Albany, the portion of the UGRR leading toward Cincinnati, outlined in detailed maps from the Adventure Cycling Association, bends away from the river and into the rolling countryside. The well-paved roads taper to a single lane with nary a car in sight and meander among midwestern hamlets, each marked by the steeple of a local church. From New Albany, the route takes you directly down Main Street in Charlestown, Indiana.

After spending two weeks in New Albany, Cummings was captured by slave catchers here in Charlestown. They took him before an Indiana judge, who sympathetically declared the law had no right to hold him. But the slave catchers were determined to get Cummings back into Kentucky. They hurried him out of the courtroom and headed south on horseback. Before reaching the Ohio, Cummings kicked one of the horses in the side and escaped into the woods—this time for good.

In Madison, the route crosses back into Kentucky, veering away from the Ohio River and into the region's hill-and-hollow topography. The smooth, narrow roads roll along vast ridgelines, with farms and fields spread to either side, then abruptly dive into densely wooded ravines, from which precipitous climbs emerge. As you ride through this sparsely populated area, you'll encounter numerous historical markers denoting the various farmhouses and hideaways that served as refuges to runaway slaves prior to their final push toward freedom—most frequently, the tiny town of Ripley, Ohio. To runaway slaves, Ripley,

Get There

▶▶ The Adventure Cycling Association's maps break the Underground Railroad Bicycle Route into easily digestible segments of 40 to 50 miles. The maps provide turn-by-turn instructions for the entirety of the route and elevation profiles to help riders determine each segment's difficulty. The locations of campgrounds, bicycle shops, and various other important travel amenities are highlighted on each map, as are the specific locations of historical sites relating to the Underground Railroad. Visit adventurecycling.org for more information.

52 miles east of Cincinnati on the northern bank of the Ohio River, was known as Freedom's Landing. Slave owners on the southern side of the Ohio called it a "hell hole of abolition." Prior to the Civil War, the quiet country roads en route to Ripley teemed with Underground Railroad activity.

As the UGRR makes its way back toward the Ohio River, it takes riders through the town of Old Washington, where today the buildings and streets remain little changed from the late 1700s. The town is a living history museum and tourist magnet. Here, you can take in tales of Underground Railroad heroes while simultaneously licking a cone filled with mint chocolate chip ice cream.

At the Paxton Inn, now restored, owner James Paxton boarded fugitive slaves in a hidden stairway between the first and second floors. Paxton was later forced to leave Washington due to his involvement with the American Colonization Society, which believed in returning slaves to Africa and was the forebearer of the country of Liberia. Down the street from the inn, the house at which Harriet Beecher Stowe, the free author of *Uncle Tom's Cabin*, stayed during a visit to Old Washington in 1833 is now a museum chronicling her experience in the town. Stowe's hosts took her to a common

> "The climb up to the Rankin house required taking a trail through the woods, clinging to roots and clutching at branches until reaching the staircase Rankin had built to allow access to his back door."

form of entertainment at the time: a slave auction held on the grassy lawn in front of the courthouse. Appalled, in her book Stowe later recounted a scene of children ripped from the arms of their mothers and grown men examined like livestock.

At the time of its publication, in 1852, *Uncle Tom's Cabin* sold more copies than any other book except for the Bible, and it is credited with creating widespread support for the antislavery movement. Stowe, who lived in Cincinnati, drew many of the book's stories and characters from incidents chronicled along the UGRR Bicycle Route.

From Old Washington, the route descends back down the river valley to Maysville, Kentucky, a modern town with historic charms, including the National

Underground Railroad Museum, a documented safe house where fugitive slaves were hidden under false floors. In Maysville, a towering suspension bridge, the first bridge east of Cincinnati, ushers travelers across the wide, green river and into Ohio.

After miles of steep hills and exhilarating descents, the ride along Scenic Byway 62 into Ripley provides a flat and relaxing end to a day of riding. The slow-moving river lies to one side, the tall, tree-lined valley ridge to the other. In the heart of Ripley, a redbrick promenade borders Front Street, where both tourists and locals dine at restaurants overlooking the Ohio River. The brick sidewalk ends at the home of John Parker, one of the Underground Railroad's most prolific conductors. Parker, born a slave in Norfolk, Virginia, purchased his own freedom by working at a steel foundry through the night. In Ripley, he started the successful Phoenix Foundry and became a prominent businessman in the community. However, his nighttime work continued. He rowed as many as 1,000 runaway slaves across the Ohio.

Once secure in Ripley, freedom-seeking slaves needed only to look to the bright light shining from the top of the valley ridge overlooking town: the home of the minister John Rankin. The brick house still stands as Ripley's proudest monument (and provides the river valley's most encompassing view). To reach the Rankin home, you'll ascend the old highway up the steep hillside—a challenging climb, yet far easier than the route taken by fugitive slaves, who were without the benefit of a bicycle. In the 1800s, the climb to the Rankin house required taking a trail through the woods below, clinging to roots and clutching at branches until reaching the staircase Rankin had built to allow access to his back door. Of the thousands that made the trek up the staircase, no slave was ever captured while sheltered by John Rankin.

The Borderland portion of the UGRR culminates with a spur into downtown Cincinnati. The ride rolls along a rail-to-trails path beside the Little Miami River, past the former home of Harriet Beecher Stowe (now the Harriet Beecher Stowe Center), and onto Freedom Way, a road connecting Cincinnati's two major sports stadiums. The nation's premier Underground Railroad museum, the Freedom Center, sits in the center of Freedom Way. Built from thick stone blocks and clad in copper, the building's undulating walls were designed to symbolize the fields and rivers fleeing slaves crossed on the journey north. Its three distinct pavilions are meant to celebrate courage, cooperation, and perseverance. Its prominent entrance is situated above the banks of the Ohio River, valiantly looking south.

Womble Trail

ARKANSAS

There's a trail in the thick woods of western Arkansas within the Ouachita National Forest that runs west to east along the ridgelines of the Ouachita Mountains. Thirty-seven miles from end to end and almost entirely composed of narrow singletrack, the Womble Trail rolls up and down rippling terrain, providing flowing descents and roller-coaster-like climbs through lofty stands of oak and pine. The trail is bench-cut across steep hillsides and crosses a tall bluff overlooking the serpentine Ouachita River.

According to the local Mount Ida Area Chamber of Commerce, the world's largest concentration of quartz crystals exists amongst the mountains and forests over which the Womble passes. And sharp-eyed riders regularly go home with pointed, translucent stones tucked into their jersey pockets, talismans of a magical ride.

Get There

▶▶ The Womble's western trailhead, at Northfork Lake, is located 48 miles west of Hot Springs, Arkansas. The Ouachita Challenge, a 60-mile mountain bike race on the Womble and surrounding trails, occurs each March. There are a number of small communities that provide lodging options near the Womble Trail, including the town of Mount Ida, the self-proclaimed Quartz Crystal Capital of the World. Visit mtidachamber.com for a list of local accommodations.

Yellowstone National Park

Though humans have inhabited this land of erupting geysers, roaring waterfalls, and gold-colored canyons for more than 11,000 years, modern American explorers didn't fully survey the area until the 1860s. When President Ulysses S. Grant signed an act of declaration in 1872 that set aside 3,468 square miles in the northwestern corner of Wyoming for the specific purpose of public appreciation, he made Yellowstone the world's first official national park.

The geologic events that created the splendor of Yellowstone, the continent's largest volcanic caldera, which certainly remains active today, occurred more than 600,000 years ago. Ancient eruptions and massive lava flows created the park's stunning scenery, as well as its 465 currently active geysers and 10,000 different geothermal features—two-thirds of the geysers in the entire world and one-half of the world's geothermal features. Every year, nearly 3.5 million tourists flock to Yellowstone to witness the eruptions of Old Faithful (generally, every 90 minutes or so), to catch glimpses of grizzly bears and bison herds, and to drive the Grand Loop, a 140-mile figure eight of park roads that takes in the most prominent attractions. Many of these visitors avoid the traffic jams spawned by wildlife-gawking drivers and discover the splendor of Yellowstone by bike.

Get There

▸▸ Yellowstone is accessible from five different entrances, on the north, northeast, east, west, and south sides of the park. A number of bus and commercial transportation providers service the park from nearby airports. Visit nps.gov/yell for more information.

When touring Yellowstone by bike, you can fill your days by spinning along the Grand Loop and overnighting in any of five different campgrounds spaced throughout the park. You can pedal dirt roads and trails that pass through backcountry scenery and lead to geysers far away from the crowds. You can ride along the banks of the Yellowstone River on an abandoned railroad bed and make the 3-mile, 1,400-foot dirt road ascent of Mount Washburn, with summit views overlooking the Yellowstone basin and stretching as far south as Grand Teton National Park. You can

> **" Ancient eruptions and massive lava flows created the park's 465 currently active geysers and 10,000 different geothermal features—two-thirds of the geysers in the entire world and one-half of the world's geothermal features."**

stop to swim in bone-chilling, high-mountain lakes and straddle your bike at the cusp of a yawning canyon, the Grand Canyon of the Yellowstone, and hear the thundering sound of an aqua blue river falling 308 feet into the belly of the gorge.

At the northern entrance to Yellowstone, in the town of Gardiner, Montana, a massive stone arch, the Roosevelt Arch, spans the road. Upon the arch's crest, an inscription reads, FOR THE BENEFIT AND ENJOYMENT OF THE PEOPLE. Every year, for a few weeks in the fall and winter, the roads beyond this arch close to cars but remain open to bicycles. And if you arrive then, after the melt or before the frost, you'll discover Yellowstone entirely for the benefit and enjoyment of people on bicycles.

The Cabot Trail

NOVA SCOTIA

This 580-kilometer ribbon of a road winds along the coast of Cape Breton Island, traversing the densely forested peaks of the Cape Breton Highlands National Park, passing through tiny fishing villages and by the occasional foraging moose, and delivering two-wheeling explorers deep into the blended cultures of the Acadian, Scottish, and native Mi'kmaq. Your days will be spent admiring the endless views of the bright-blue bays and sheer cliffsides as you ride an endless series of climbs and descents—including a number of grades above 15 percent—rising and falling along the island's rugged shoreline. Afternoons and evenings bring delectable refueling options, with fresh clam chowder and lobster feasts. Whether you camp in the array of parks or opt for the variety of locally owned bed-and-breakfasts along the route, you'll find that on this wild island, salmon leap from streams, whales patrol the bays, and cyclists rule the roads.

Get There

▶▶ The Nova Scotian cities of Halifax and Sydney host the airports closest to the Cabot Trail's jumping-off point, the tiny fishing village of Baddeck. Touring groups such as Freewheeling Adventures (freewheeling.ca) provide fully supported and self-guided tours on the Cabot Trail, while the Vélo Max bicycle shop in the town of Chéticamp caters to the many self-supported bike tourists. It's recommended that riders pack light due to the challenging terrain and reserve accommodations in advance during the Cabot Trail's peak season, June through September. Visit novascotia.com to acquire detailed maps of the Cabot Trail and for more information about lodging and dining options along the route.

Icefields Parkway

ALBERTA

Running alongside the spine of the Continental Divide, the Icefields Parkway spans the Canadian Rocky Mountains Parks World Heritage Site in the province of Alberta. Riding the parkway south, from Jasper toward Banff, you'll pedal toward glacier-encrusted peaks, past mirrorlike lakes, and through the Columbia Icefield, a sheet of ice covering 325 square kilometers.

Get There

▸▸ The ride between Jasper and Banff is 307 kilometers, two-thirds of which is on the official Icefields Parkway. Just outside Jasper, many cyclists choose to detour onto the Old Icefields Parkway, a quieter stretch of road that parallels the main route for 24 kilometers. The Icefields Parkway terminates in the town of Lake Louise, and the Bow Valley Parkway, a scenic stretch of road that's mostly car free, continues another 70 kilometers south to Banff. The closest major airport is in Calgary, 127 kilometers east of Banff. A number of touring companies offer fully supported multiday cycling trips along the Icefields Parkway. Visit icefieldsparkway.ca for more information on accommodations along the route.

Seven Summits

BRITISH COLUMBIA

Just across the US border, tucked tightly into the Canadian Rockies of British Columbia, sits an old gold-mining town called Rossland. Though the mines dried up long ago, today there's still treasure in the steep mountainsides bordering Rossland on all sides. The self-proclaimed mountain biking capital of Canada, Rossland has spent hundreds of thousands of dollars cultivating a world-class trail system. The result is an international mountain biking destination and one of the most celebrated 1-day epics in the world.

In 1999 the Kootenay Columbia Trails Society began work on a point-to-point route traversing the ridgeline of the Rossland Range, summiting seven different mountains via 30 kilometers of pure fat-tire singletrack. Completed in 2004, the resulting ride has been honored as an official epic by the International Mountain Biking Association and was named the trail of the year by *Bike* magazine in 2007.

The Seven Summits trail starts in a gravelly parking oval off Highway 3B, 20 kilometers north of Rossland. As you dip into the dense forest, a steep switchback climb rises more than 600 meters over 6.5 kilometers. Near the crest of the climb, the trees thin, allowing a moment to catch your breath while taking in panoramic views of the undulating mountain range and the

> **Get There**
>
> ▸▸ Though riding the highway out to the trailhead of the Seven Summits and taking Highway 22 for 9 kilometers back to town after the descent of the Dewdney Trail is certainly doable, most riders opt to shuttle the start and finish of the ride. Various shuttle services and guides are available in Rossland. Visit rosslandtrails.ca for more information.

pointed, gray peak of Old Glory to the southwest. Ahead lie 2,135 meters of descent back toward Rossland, along exposed ridgelines and bench-cut trails, interspersed with another 762 meters of undulating climbs. On the Seven Summits, every awe-inspiring downhill is earned.

The trail culminates with a flowing 7-kilometer run down the Dewdney Trail, which isn't officially part of the Seven Summits trail but might as well be, for only the foolish would take the optional dirt road back to Rossland rather than spend the last 20 to 30 minutes of their ride flowing down a descent that drops more than 600 meters in just 5.5 kilometers.

Some might argue that the Seven Summits trail doesn't actually summit seven peaks. It hugs the ridgelines and contours of the mountains rather than going all the way up and down. These people are missing the point. The trail's name comes from the mountain peaks it bypasses, but it is also a play on mountain climbers' quests to bag the seven summits that are the highest peaks on every continent. Sure, maybe it's not Everest or Mount McKinley, but on the Seven Summits trail, at times you'll feel as if you're on top of the world—and by sunset, you'll be enjoying a cold beer.

"The self-proclaimed mountain biking capital of Canada, Rossland has spent hundreds of thousands of dollars cultivating a world-class trail system."

UNITED STATES

MEXICO

MEXICO

Copper Canyon

Like long, gnarled fingers, the canyons cut deep swaths through the plateaus, mesas, and peaks of the Sierra Madre Occidental in the Mexican state of Chihuahua. Half a dozen or more (depending on who's counting) cavernous gorges situated adjacent to one another, all carved by rivers sluicing through auburn-hued rock and plunging more than 1,800 meters from abrupt ledges to the valley floor, together make up the mystical land known as Copper Canyon.

The Tarahumara live here, as they've done for centuries, somehow surviving the various conquering empires, the Aztecs and the conquistadores and the modern-day drug lords. Today, rough population counts put the Tarahumara at 106,000 people scattered across the canyons, many still adhering to the traditions of their ancestors. Their homes are huts built into cliff walls. Their religious ceremonies are fueled by homemade corn brew. Their sport is nonstop running races that can last for days.

This tribe has long fascinated outsiders and intermittently grabbed moments of fame for its long-distance running exploits. In 1994, Tarahumara runners appeared on national television clad in bright robes and rubber sandals, trotting to victory at the Leadville ultra-endurance race, an off-road, 100-mile course through the high Rockies that follows a route similar to the popular mountain bike event (page 138) but on foot. And in 2009, in the bestselling book *Born to Run,* author Chris McDougall sought to unlock the mystery of the Tarahumara's knack for running such long distances without ever getting hurt.

The Tarahumara run out of necessity rather than an inherent love of physical fitness. Running, for these people, is simply a means of getting from one point to another. There's little modern infrastructure in the remote crevices of Copper Canyon, no electricity or plumbing or roads, and many villages sit kilometers apart. Thus, the Tarahumara have long relied on a vast trail system as a primary means of transportation, a network of rudimentary paths spanning the canyon ledges, cliffsides, and winding river basins.

Get There

▶▶ Foreigners who visit Copper Canyon typically fly into Chihuahua City, 160 miles northeast of Creel, or drive down from El Paso, Texas, 391 miles to the north. Katun Tours offers multiday guided mountain bike trips in the Creel and Copper Canyons, including lodging and shuttle service. Visit katuntours.com for more information.

The first groups of mountain bikers arrived in Copper Canyon in the 1980s and soon discovered that the trails of the Tarahumara and the dirt roads that switchback down the sheer canyon walls make for incomparable riding. Knobby-tired adventures here typically start in the town of Creel, known as the gateway to Copper Canyon. Rafael Camposeco Gonzalez, who runs guided mountain bike trips in the region through his business, Katun Tours, says that on just the dry, rock-strewn mountains surrounding Creel, above the canyons, "you could easily spend a week riding magnificent singletrack." But the true splendor comes on the nearly 60-kilometer ride down a single-lane dirt road to the bottom of La Bufa, one of the deepest canyons, and the town of Batopilas on the banks of a river by the same name. On the dramatic descent into the canyon, every turn exposes new and ever more stunning views of sun-tinted rock formations, shimmering in the shade of the precious metal for which the canyon system got its name, and green foliage that thickens into a tropical jungle as the road nears the Batopilas River. The once-grand mining enclave now welcomes two-wheeling tourists with restaurants and lodging and more trails that lead to historic missions and towering waterfalls and border an ancient aqueduct that still collects and carries the canyon's clear waters.

Any way you choose to pedal out of the canyon requires ascending hundreds of meters. Most riders choose not to hitch a ride with a guide service–provided shuttle and instead take on more than 5 hours of climbing to the nearest paved road. The task may seem daunting, but then again, consider yourself lucky—you have a bike. If you were a native of Copper Canyon, a Tarahumara, well, you'd just run there.

South America

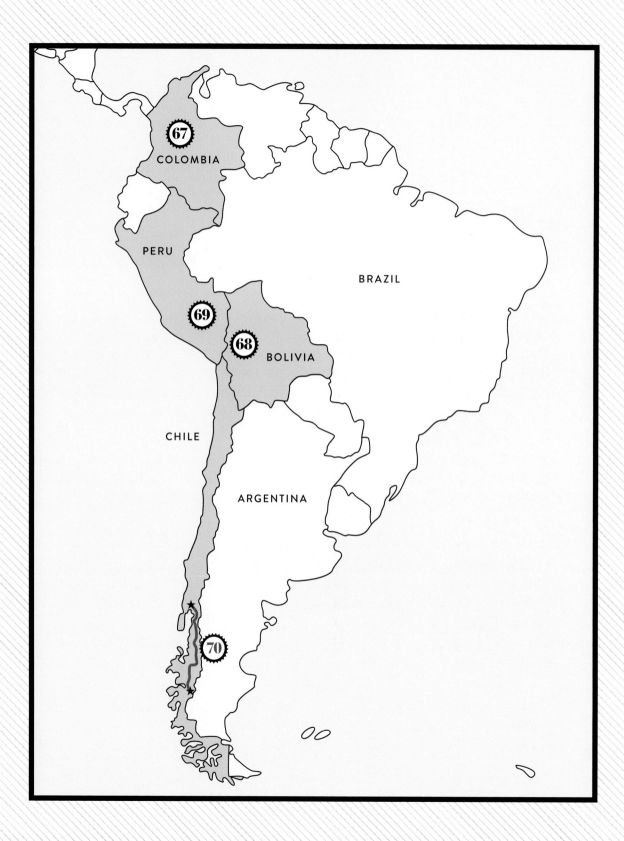

Alto de Letras

COLOMBIA

The first set of hairpin turns on what's often referred to as the world's longest mountain climb arrives less than a kilometer after leaving the tiny village of Mariquita, Columbia, and crossing the Rio Gualí. The turns wiggle back on one another like an earthworm pried from the soil. The asphalt is smooth. The corners gently banked. The gradient a mild 6 percent.

At this early point, after clearing these initial turns, the road to Alto de Letras—the most mythic ascent in a country where cycling, climbing, in particular, has been mythologized to the point of religion—has already risen 46 meters. Another 960 meters of continuous climbing remain.

As the road rises along the 80.5 kilometers from the valley floor in Mariquita toward the highest peak in Colombia's Central Andres,

Get There

▶▶ Mariquita is a 4-hour drive west of Bogotá and 5.5 hours south of Medellín. There are various hotels and restaurants in Mariquita. After summiting Letras, most riders descend 29 kilometers into Manizales, a university city and the hub of Colombia's coffee industry.

Nevado del Ruiz, thick, green foliage presses in from all sides, a jungle of leafy ferns that form a sun-stifling canopy of squawking birds and buzzing insects. The air is thick, moist, and hot—very hot. This land, bisected by the equator, knows no seasons. Only height determines climate. Here, near sea level, it's an endless summer.

Those who embark on the ascent of Letras must come prepared for a full day of riding uphill. The fastest-ever time up the mountain, recorded in 2007 during the Vuelta a Colombia, the country's national tour, by Santiago Botero, a former world champion (known to have benefited from pharmacological assistance), is a mind-boggling 3.5 hours. Mortals should plan on 5 to 6 hours of climbing.

The air thins as you ascend, with the temperature shifting from near 32°C at the base of the mountain to 5°C to 7°C in the thin air at the peak, a treeless, windswept plateau. Small towns that dot the route to the summit are sources for a coffee, pastry, or reinvigorating soda. But mostly, the climb up Alto de Letras is composed of

The climb up Alto de Letras is composed of vast stretches of nothingness. Nothing but the Andean peaks stretching out to either side, eerily shrouded by mist and draped in a blanket of green.

vast stretches of nothingness. Nothing but the Andean peaks stretching out to either side, eerily shrouded by mist and draped in a blanket of green. Nothing but the road, ever-winding before you. Nothing but the heaving sound of your own strained lungs.

When the locals spot you, they'll wave, whistle, clap, for they know precisely what you're doing, and why you're doing it. Cars and trucks will give you a wide berth and perhaps a tap of the horn for encouragement. Children may run or ride alongside you, racing. In Colombia, it is not baseball or basketball or even soccer, in soccer-mad South America, that is the national sport. It is bike racing.

It was cycling, and in particular the Vuelta a Colombia, that brought a divided and disparate nation together in the 1980s, during a period of violent political conflict and desolation. And it was stars like Lucho Herrera, one of the so-called *escarabajos* ("flying beetles"), who introduced Colombian cycling to the world when he won a mountainous stage of the Tour de France in 1984 and gave Colombians a reason to celebrate collectively. Today, Colombia has a whole new set of stars, with diminutive climbers like Nairo Quintana ripping apart the (comparatively short) Alpine and Pyrenean ascents of the Tour de France, but Lucho Herrera remains a godlike figure in the deeply Catholic country.

When asked to expound upon the nation's obsession with cycling, Klaus Bellon, who runs the Colombian-focused bike racing Web site Alps and Andes, theorized that the roots of Colombian cycling are, in fact, grounded in its religion. Bellon says, "Colombians really respond to the idea of martyrdom, to the extent that some of the biggest churches in Bogotá do not have Christ on a cross because that's simply not painful enough. Rather, he's on the floor with the cross on his shoulders, bloodied. I think that the Colombian mentality responds to the idea of pain and martyrdom that is apparent in cycling, but climbing in particular, which is a lone struggle. Several articles from 1984 to '87 in major Colombian newspapers reference Lucho Herrera as a Christ figure, bloodied. They refer to him as a *crucis,* a cross. In a very biblical way, they see the Stations of the Cross as someone climbing a mountain. Perhaps that's journalists taking liberties with iconography and terminology that people will understand, but I do think there's something about the Colombian mind-set that responds to that image of pain and struggle that's so inherent in cycling, and now gets completely overblown."

So as you ascend toward the volcanic peaks of the Andes, within view of the semidormant Nevado del Ruiz, which is known to spew occasional plumes of ash, don't be surprised if someone leans out the window of a car, and shouts, *"Venga, Lucho!"* For this is a truly mythic mountain climb (the longest in the world, they say), in a country where the national identity is deeply tied to the suffering cycling inflicts.

Camino del Muerte

BOLIVIA

White roadside crosses mark the spots where more than a dozen cyclists and hundreds of motorists have perished descending North Yungas Road, deep in the Amazon jungle. The narrow dirt road cuts along treacherous Andean cliffsides and drops nearly 3,660 meters over 65 kilometers, from the thin air of La Paz down into a lush rain forest and the town of Coroico. Yet, in spite of the ominous landmarks—and the exposed edges of the treacherous road that drop off hundreds of meters into a misty oblivion—hordes of mountain bikers take off down the "Road of Death" every year, seeking thrills and taunting their own mortality.

Get There

▶▶ With an increase in professional tour operators and a new bypass that funnels auto traffic to the opposite side of the valley, the ride down Yungas is slightly less perilous than in the past, but extreme caution is obviously advised. Tour company Gravity Assisted Mountain Biking has one of the best safety reputations due to its well-maintained dual-suspension mountain bikes and guides trained in performing rope rescues. Visit gravitybolivia.com for more information.

CAMINO DEL MUERTE

The Inca Trail

PERU

The ancient Inca Empire considered these mountains sacred. In the craggy, cloud-strewn peaks of the high Andes, they built elaborate living monuments in honor of their fiercest warriors and greatest chiefs. By the 15th century the Inca Empire stretched across the Andes, from the top of South America down into modern-day Argentina, and the road system connecting it all, an expansive network of highly engineered paths, spanned an estimated 40,000 kilometers. Centuries after its construction, much of the Inca Trail network remains in nearly pristine condition, and in the heart of their empire—today, Peru—you'll find some of the world's most incredible mountain bike rides.

Peru's most-renowned singletrack adventure is the Olleros Trail, a 55-kilometer all-mountain ride from high up in the Andes back down to sandy Pacific Ocean beaches in Punta Negra, just outside the capital city of Lima. Riding the Olleros Trail starts early in the day, with a 3-hour shuttle ride on a precipitously narrow Andean highway to a small town more than 3,350 meters above the Pacific. At the trailhead, the 3-hour return trip begins. The trail starts with a flowing ridgeline ride along sparsely vegetated mountain slopes, a sea of mountain peaks that look like golden waves disappearing into the

Get There

▶▶ A variety of companies provide guided tours and other travel services to help you ride Peru's best mountain biking trails. Sacred Rides, routinely rated one of the best outfitters by national travel magazines, offers a variety of 10-day mountain biking trips in Peru. Visit sacredrides.com for more information.

distant horizon, then drops into a dry riverbed valley, the mountains now rising around you from all sides. Those who've descended the Olleros Trail describe riding in a dreamlike state, consumed by disbelief that singletrack like this could exist in such a remote and stunning location.

Far deeper into the Andes from the Olleros Trail, the area surrounding the Incan capital of Cusco offers similarly jaw-dropping rides. The expansive network of trails winds down lush green mountainsides, along exposed ledges and rushing riverbeds, and past ancient Incan ruins—villages, temples, and agricultural sites built from stone, still standing after more than 500 years.

Ride the trails the Incas built and you'll truly come to understand the sacred nature of these mountains.

"The Inca Empire stretched across the Andes, and the road system connecting it all, an expansive network of highly engineered paths, spanned an estimated 40,000 kilometers."

Carretera Austral

CHILE

Way down deep at the southern tip of the inhabited world, a single road slices through mountainous, remote, sublime Patagonia. Over 1,200 kilometers, the Carretera Austral, Chile's Route 7, traverses a landscape of snowcapped volcanoes, calving glaciers, and pristine lakes. Lush rain forests dominate the northern end of the route, starting in Puerto Montt. Here, the road—in parts paved, in parts gravel—is canopied by trees and enshrouded by ferns. Waterfalls tumble down tree-laden mountainsides and pool in aqua-hued rivers. Roughly past the midpoint, in the town of Coyhaique, the climate turns more temperate, and the coarse peaks stripped of vegetation and valleys open up into golden, grassy tundra. Granite spires cast epic shadows across the road, and narrow bridges span the tips of ice-blue glacial lakes. Riding the Carretera Austral requires making three different ferry passages of these finger-shaped lakes.

Construction began on the Carretera Austral in 1976, under the dictatorship of Augusto Pinochet, but wasn't completed until 2000, when it finally reached Villa O'Higgins, a popular launch point for trekking expeditions into the Southern Patagonia Icefield.

Get There

▸▸ It's recommended that you ride the Carretera Austral from north to south to take advantage of the prevailing winds. Many travelers arrive in Puerto Montt by plane from Santiago. Returning from Villa O'Higgins can be done by bus, chartered flight, or a combination of bus, flight, and ferry. Some cyclists continue farther south to El Chaltén in Argentina, crossing the border via a rugged singletrack trail. For more information on the dams threatening Patagonia, visit sinrepresas.com.

To build the route, it took the collective efforts of 10,000 men from the Chilean Army's Engineering Command (many of whom lost their lives and are memorialized with white roadside markers), yet the area remains almost entirely uninhabited. Today, only about 100,000 people live along the roadway. As it is one of the most cherished rides amongst adventurous bike tourists, it's common to meet other

> **The road—in parts paved, in parts gravel—is canopied by trees and enshrouded by ferns. Waterfalls tumble down tree-laden mountainsides and pool in aqua-hued rivers.**

cyclists along the Carretera Austral, but the road in its undisturbed form may soon cease to exist. A series of ambitious dam projects in Patagonia proposed by the Chilean government would funnel hydroelectric power to the more densely populated northern part of the country and bring trucks toting heavy equipment to the Carretera Austral. Hillsides would be cleared of trees and rock faces blasted to route power lines. There's strong opposition to the dam projects from the organization Patagonia Sin Represas ("Patagonia Without Dams") and a variety of ways to assist in preserving the region. However, one simple way to raise awareness is to go ride the Carretera Austral yourself and share the splendor of this incredible place.

United Kingdom

ISLE OF SKYE

7Stanes

SCOTLAND

The giant stones sit heavily in the damp woods and mossy glens of the Scottish countryside. Cut from hunks of quartz, granite, and marble, they weigh as much as 6 tons and stand as tall as 3 meters. Each stone is carved to capture the lore and legend of the land in which it resides, places such as Glentress, Mabie, Dalbeattie, and Ae. Representing a ghost and an extraterrestrial, the head of a giant's broken ax and a hidden gem, the massive sculptures adorn seven different mountain biking centers known as the 7Stanes that are spread throughout the forest preserves of southern Scotland.

Since the early 2000s, with financial and logistical support from the country's Forestry Commission, professional trail builders have cut hundreds of kilometers of world-class singletrack that cater to a wide array of off-road disciplines and ability levels. Every trail is graded for its difficulty, from beginners' green trails to experts' black, and range from long-distance cross-country routes that dip and dive along the contours of the countryside to freeride courses filled with berms, rock drops, jumps, and wall ramps.

At the Dalbeattie Slab, you'll peer across a lush valley before plunging down the face of an inconceivably sheer granite drop. On the Edge trail in Ae, you'll trace the

Get There

▸▸ An array of bike shops, outfitters, cafés, and accommodations has sprouted up in the small villages in which the 7Stanes are located. Visit 7stanesmountainbiking.com for more information.

open lip of a deep gorge high above a rushing river. In the freeride park at Glentress, you'll find three timber ladder drops called the Hucks and a 2.5-meter-high, 4.5-meter-long jump called the Funbox.

You'll also discover the stones that mark each of the 7Stanes and help tell their stories far out on the rocky, rooted, twisting trails in the south of Scotland.

C2C

ENGLAND

Every year at the Whitehaven harbor, on the shore of the Irish Sea, thousands of cyclists stand beside a tall, steel statue vertically inscribed with the acronym C2C and dip the rear wheels of their bicycles into the dark water. Then, they embark on a cycling journey that's come to define Britain. This journey, 140 miles from the island's western coast to its eastern coast on the Red Sea, begins here, by this statue, often with a photo and tidings of good luck and safe passage.

Officially known as the Sea to Sea route, this ride across the width of Britain, ending in the city of Newcastle, isn't the toughest or longest cross-country ride in the United Kingdom. There's the well-known ride lengthwise, from Lands End to John O'Groats, and a similar coast-to-coast ride across the width of Britain that's almost entirely on dirt roads and paths. However, since its creation by the nonprofit transportation advocacy group Sustrans in 1994, the C2C has gained immense popularity, attracting as many as 15,000 riders annually, and become the most iconic bicycle trip in all the United Kingdom—a cultural rite of passage for both hard-core cyclists and the general populace.

The route rolls north along the coast from Whitehaven before turning to the east, placing the prevailing winds at your back. From the coast of the Irish Sea, you'll

> ## Get There
>
> ▸▸ With thousands of riders annually taking on the C2C, a number of bed-and-breakfasts and restaurants have sprung up along the route. Additionally, a variety of outfitters and charity challenges offer fully supported trips along the C2C. Visit sustrans.org for comprehensive maps and more information about the route.

pass through the Lake District National Park and cross the Pennines mountain range. You'll climb nearly to the very "roof of Britain," at 580 meters above sea level, with the ascent of Hartside Pass, atop which sits the Hartside Café, famous for its baked goods, sweeping views of the grassy mountains, and self-proclaimed status as Britain's highest restaurant. On the C2C, you'll ride on a roughly 50 percent mixture of quiet country lanes and car-free paths made from converted railways, with numerous tunnels, trestles, and viaducts along the route.

Near its terminus, the C2C splits in two and officially ends in both Newcastle and Sunderland, where it's tradition—naturally—to dip a tire into the cold Red Sea.

"**Since its creation in 1994, the C2C has attracted as many as 15,000 riders annually, and become the most iconic bicycle trip in all of the United Kingdom—a cultural rite of passage for both hard-core cyclists and the general populace.**"

Isle of Skye

SCOTLAND

The dark volcanic rock rises from the surrounding green slopes in towering spires and sheer cliffs, forming a 30.5-kilometer ridge down the center of the Trotternish peninsula on Scotland's Isle of Skye. The rock formations on this rustic isle have long inspired Gaelic legend and even Hollywood directors (Ridley Scott shot his 2012 film *Prometheus* here), and they have also drawn cyclists from across the United Kingdom and around the world.

An 80-kilometer loop starting in the town of Portree runs along the edge of the peninsula, through rolling farm fields, and between the shore of the Atlantic and the looming ridgeline. You'll first encounter the Old Man of Storr, a knifelike outcrop that rises more than 600 meters above the nearby sea. Local folklore tells of a giant who sank into the earth here, leaving only his thumb pointing toward the sky. More likely, lava, battered by thousands of years of wind, rain, and erosion, formed the Storr.

Farther down the a single-lane road snakes up and over the ridge of a beguiling rock formation known as Quiraing. Here, grassy plateaus appear to be held above the surrounding sea by sheer walls of stone. Nearby, turrets of basalt known as the Needle and the Prison rise imposingly from the earth. It's said early inhabitants shielded their cattle from Viking invaders behind these tall outcroppings.

Get There

▸▸ Glasgow, 345 kilometers south of Portree, is the closest international airport to the Isle of Skye. A number of outfitters in Portree offer bicycle rentals. Visit isleofskye.com for information on accommodations on the Trotternish peninsula.

Various Locations

The Bicycle Film Festival

People who like bicycles—really like bicycles—have a problem. See, it's not enough for these people to ride bicycles, and buy bicycles, and work on bicycles, and talk about bicycles incessantly. No, in addition, they must read about bicycles, listen to songs about bicycles, and put paintings of bicycles on their walls. In every facet of their lives, bicycles consume them. To be fair, it's not just bicyclists who suffer from this sort of obsessive affliction. Surfers do, too. And skiers.

Get There

▸▸ Visit bicyclefilmfestival.com and Facebook.com/BicycleFilmFestival for tour dates and details.

When a sport outgrows the activity itself, it becomes a way of life, a cultural phenomenon that cultivates passion and inspires creativity. Of course, if you are one of these people, this obsession is not a problem at all. It is a blessing. Because around the world, there are other people who feel equal affection for bicycling, and some of these people are filmmakers. Filmmakers who make beautiful films about bicycles—well, the films have bicycles in them, at least, even if they're often more about life than about bicycles—who submit these films to the Bicycle Film Festival.

If you live in one of the 30 (and counting) cities to which the Bicycle Film Festival makes its annual pilgrimage, or if you're willing to travel to, say, New York or San Francisco, or even Warsaw or Istanbul or Tokyo, then you will see some of the finest films featuring bicycles ever made. Films about physical suffering, about adventure in faraway worlds, about falling in (and out of) love, about friends and happiness, and evil and good, and about having fun—just, fun.

In these films, there are bikes of all types, knobby-tired and fixed-geared and small-wheeled, and outside the theater—usually some offbeat artsy venue—you will see all of these different types of bikes, too, chained to racks in thick piles. You will see bicyclists of every age and gender and fashion standing in a long line, chatting casually, probably about bikes, with the sense of anxious excitement that tends to fill the air outside movie theaters where long lines form.

Then the doors open. Tickets are taken. Drinks are poured. Popcorn is served. All the people who've come to watch movies about bikes take their seats, and the founder of the Bicycle Film Festival, Brendt Barbur, stands before the assembled

> **"You will see bicyclists of every age and gender and fashion standing in a long line, chatting casually, probably about bikes, with the sense of anxious excitement that tends to fill the air outside movie theaters where long lines form."**

audience and makes an introduction. Barbur started the festival in 2001 after he was doored on his bike and thrown into the path of a New York City bus, because he wanted something positive for bicycles to come from his accident. So when he speaks to the assembled audience of bicyclists about the hundreds of submissions from which these few films, both shorts and features, have been selected, he speaks, also, as someone who really loves bicycles. He reminds everyone in attendance about the after parties, the social bike rides, the live music and DJs that make up the festive part of the Bicycle Film Festival.

Then, Barbur exits the stage, the lights dim, the film flickers onto the screen, and finally, for all the people in attendance who really like bicycles, the show begins.

The Cyclocross World Championships

VARIOUS LOCATIONS

Amidst the mud and the beer, the blaring horns, and the ludicrous costumes, the cowbell stands out. Big and shiny and clangy. Silly, not entirely unlike the cycling discipline for which it rings: cyclocross, a wintertime mash-up of road racing and mountain biking often taking place in horrendous weather over a circuitous course that's littered with large obstacles requiring racers to dismount and run up and over to surmount them.

When attending a cyclocross race, you might ask, "Why the cowbell?" Further, what motivates men and women to dress in skintight outfits, rub shiny embrocation on their bare legs, and ride around on (and run with) bikes in subfreezing temperatures as fast as they can for an hour? Is it wrong to take pleasure in witnessing the agony of world-class athletes? Will I burn off the calories in this bratwurst and basket of frites if I scream loud enough or shake this cowbell even more vigorously?

You may find the answers to these questions—and many more—only by attending a cyclocross race in person. And the races above all races to see in person, in all of cycling—heck, in all of sports—are the Cyclocross World Championships.

Consider this: In Belgium, the nation in which the anaerobic heart of cyclocross beats, the world championships are bigger than the Super Bowl. The 2012 Cyclocross World Championship in Koksijde, Belgium, sold out with 68,500 ticket-buying fans (who also consumed 30,000 liters of Jupiter beer). At the Super Bowl in Indianapolis that same year, there were 68,000 live spectators. Based on the percentage of households tuning in to the event, the ratings for the TV broadcast of the Cyclocross World Championships in Belgium, were nearly double the ratings for the Super Bowl in the United States.

That Belgian fervor for cyclocross is spreading worldwide, especially to the States. Between 2005 and 2011, the number of cyclocross racers in the United States tripled in size, and in 2012, the country held more internationally sanctioned cyclocross events than any other country in the world. In February 2013, the world championship of cyclocross took place in the United States, in the sticky bluegrass mud of Louisville—the first time the race was held outside Europe in its 63-year history.

On a course laid out along the banks of the Ohio River, American fans displayed the full, ridiculous extent of their nascent passion for cyclocross. Groups of grown men dressed in matching superhero costumes. Elderly women painted their faces. Young, beautiful people of both sexes bared their midriffs as snow flurries swirled around them and waved glitter-adorned placards in support of their favorite racers, the Belgian "General" Sven Nys and American star Katie "F'n" Compton. (Both of whom later stated that Belgian fans could learn a thing or two from the level of enthusiasm Americans bring to cyclocross races.)

Crescendos of heckling, a form of anti-cheering endorsed by Belgian cyclocross fanatics but taken to new levels of sarcastic absurdity by the wittiest of American superfans, rained from the racecourse's packed sidelines. Hands beat the course barriers like a giant, continuous drumroll, and a cacophony

Get There

▸▸ The Cyclocross World Championships will take place in Heusden-Zolder, Belgium, in 2016. Visit UCI.ch for event and accommodation information.

of horns accompanied the ubiquitous chorus of clanging cowbells, along with the Christopher Walken–coined refrain "More cowbell!"

Perhaps the only part of the Cyclocross World Championships that's more compelling than the sea of raucous spectators is the actual race. Earth's best cyclocross racers display an incredible combination of fitness and bike-handling skills, sprinting away from the line in a mass pack and maintaining that all-out speed through treacherous sandpits, mud-slick descents, and run-ups so steep the racers often paw at the ground in front of them while hoisting their bikes uphill.

Yes, there are bigger bike races and wilder parties to attend, but no other event offers the same insane level of revelry and masochistic competition as the Cyclocross World Championships—and the event needs more cowbell, from you.

Acknowledgments

A work of nonfiction is the sum of its sources, and to all the individuals who shared with me their own bucket lists—their personal dreams and cycling aspirations—I am eternally grateful. This book would not have been possible without the help of these adventurers, local experts, and world travelers, with whom I spent hours speaking. The sources for *The Cyclist's Bucket List* patiently led me to understand the experiences chronicled here, as experienced through their eyes. I wish many thanks, and many future adventures, to these generous bicyclists.

Index

Boldface page references indicate photos and maps. <u>Underscored</u> references indicate boxed text.

Photo Credits